Also by Arthur B. Laffer

Taxes Have Consequences: An Income Tax History of the United States

Also by Stephen Moore

Govzilla: How the Relentless Growth of Government Is Devouring Our Economy—And Our Freedom

THE TRUMP ECONOMIC MIRACLE

AND THE PLAN TO UNLEASH PROSPERITY AGAIN

ARTHUR B.
LAFFER, Ph.D.
& STEPHEN
MOORE

A POST HILL PRESS BOOK
ISBN: 979-8-89565-004-2
ISBN (eBook): 979-889565-005-9

The Trump Economic Miracle:
And the Plan to Unleash Prosperity Again

This book, as well as any other Post Hill Press publications, may be purchased in bulk quantities at a special discounted rate. Contact orders@posthillpress.com for more information.

This is a work of nonfiction. All people, locations, events, and situations are portrayed to the best of the author's memory.

Post Hill Press
New York • Nashville
posthillpress.com

Published in the United States of America
1 2 3 4 5 6 7 8 9 10

DEDICATED TO THOSE WHO CAME BEFORE

TABLE OF CONTENTS

FOREWORD

by Donald J. Trump

My first term as President of the United States was filled with achievements, including secure borders, low inflation, economic growth, peace through American strength, and a Supreme Court that respects the Constitution. The cornerstone of my administration's success was my redesign of our economic policy, especially the Tax Cuts and Jobs Act (TCJA) of 2017. I had many advisors and staff working to craft the tax cuts, but the authors of this book, Stephen Moore and Arthur Laffer, were the driving force, along with, of course, my waiting-in-the-wings head of the National Economic Council, Larry Kudlow. Without their knowledge and insight into the American tax code, we'd have never been able to enact the largest tax cut ever. Here is what we got done in office:

1) The Tax Cuts and Jobs Act was committed to finding the most damaging parts of our tax code and correcting them. The TCJA:
   a) identified the most harmful marginal tax rate—our corporate rate was the highest in the

world—and I cut it by 40 percent, from 35 all the way down to 21 percent.

b) cut the highest personal income tax rate from 39.6 to 37 percent.

c) made capital-equipment expensing immediate.

d) curbed state and local tax deductions.

The TCJA was enacted in my first year and its provisions were effective immediately. Even the greatest tax-rate-cutters, my inspirational predecessors Ronald Reagan and John F. Kennedy didn't implement their tax plans so quickly.

2) The executive order on healthcare price transparency enabled Americans, at last, to see what they are paying for healthcare beforehand and stood up to surprise billing. Our legislation on right-to-try not only provided hope to the terminally ill, but accelerated medical innovation. And the rollout of a COVID-19 vaccine in 11 months was nothing short of a miracle. The research it engendered, especially in the field of mRNA, is still saving lives.

3) Energy policy was first-order amazing. We freed up oil and gas production, and America became energy-independent for the first time since the 1950s. As far as immigration goes, in the best traditions of this country we welcomed those who aspire to make it in America legally, and we kept out the "bad hombres." We secured the border.

4) The Supreme Court picks were stellar. The Court has now begun, and is in a position to continue, reigning in unelected, congressionally unauthorized impositions of new and expanded restrictions,

requirements, and rules that harm our economy and are an affront to our rule of law. The decision of earlier this year against the "Chevron doctrine" (the doctrine enabling bureaucrats to make law) is an example. In his opinion, my Court appointment Neil Gorsuch wrote, "today, the Court places a tombstone on Chevron no one can miss."

5) Our trade agreements were wonderful. I was, as I will always be, open to freer and fairer trade when agreed to by both nations. But I will never let foreigners exploit American workers.
6) And lastly, when America gets its economic policy right, the world simmers down. The defense posture and foreign policy of my administration were amazingly successful. No wars, historic international reconciliations, the Abraham Accords and the move of Israel's capital to Jerusalem, as well as the rapprochement with Kim Jong Un. When I was president and putting in my policies, there were no wars because of my policies and because of American leadership.

More specifically, I am especially proud our how the TCJA stacks up against the history of the best tax cuts of the past. We cut taxes right away in our first year, with no delays in implementation. It was a first in American history:

1) In the 1920s, tax-rate cuts were staggered. Warren Harding got the first tax cut in 1922, taking the top rate down from 73 percent to 58 percent. The next two tax-rate cuts came under Calvin Coolidge and

took time. The top rate fell to 25 percent only in 1925. America got its tax cuts and with them the roaring twenties, but it was a slog, legislatively. I was pleased to get mine all at once.

2) In 1948, Harry Truman wished to keep the super-high World War II era tax structure and vetoed a big tax-rate cut. Congress had the good sense to override the veto. Under my leadership, Congress supported my tax cuts.
3) John F. Kennedy in the early 1960s took the full thousand days of his cut-short presidency to get his tax-reduction bill near passage. Even then, it took sympathy from the assassination and Lyndon Johnson's insistence for the tax cut to become law in 1964, three years after JFK's inauguration. The delay in cutting taxes caused the stock market to fall by 30 percent. We did not delay tax cuts, and the economy responded magnificently.
4) And then in the early 1980s, Reagan's tax cut was phased-in, and the highest tax rate on earned income was not lowered. The Reagan recession of 1981-82 was horrible, as the administration waited for the law it passed to take full effect. This was followed in 1983 by an economic expansion of unprecedented proportions. Even so, in 1984, a healthy majority of the Cabinet urged Reagan to raise tax rates to higher levels than were in effect in the 1960s (the president declined). We did not make any of these mistakes. We cut taxes once and for all right away.

In contrast to these examples, my TCJA was wrapped up before my first year in the White House was over. There is nothing like this in income-tax-cut policy history.

When we speak of successful presidencies, invariably they were two-term presidencies in which a mid-course correction took place in the first term after mistakes. (The classic example is Bill Clinton.) The successes of 2017-19 happened without retracement and re-trying. I got the big-ticket items right the first time. It is uncanny how few examples of such success the history of the presidency offers.

As for whether the economic statistics were historic—this book documents that in many ways they were. The entrenched rate of growth in the economy had been sub-2 percent from 2000-2016. My administration sustained an increase well above that. Furthermore, the pushing 3 percent growth of 2018-19 also occurred very late in an economic expansion, one dating from the recovery from the 2008 recession. Business cycle theory says that growth should fall so late in an expansion. Yet growth accelerated when we enacted my tax cuts. Before those tax cuts, the United States had been lagging Europe. After, it sported a higher rate of growth. And if those accomplishments are not enough, my Tax Cuts and Jobs Act actually paid for itself as revenues soared thanks to higher growth and more workers working than ever before. Critics, put that in your pipe and smoke it.

This book belongs to Arthur Laffer and Steve Moore. I can't endorse all the ideas and proposals in this book as my own platform, but the policies espoused by Art and Steve have been and continue to be my guiding light when making economic policy decisions.

—Donald J. Trump

PREFACE

How Donald Trump Will Make America Great Again...Again

In late August of 2023, President Donald Trump contacted us to meet with him at his country club/summer compound in New Jersey. This was a bit of a *déjà vu* for the two of us, as it reminded us of our first meeting with Trump back in early 2016—the first time Trump ran for the White House.

At that time the two of us, along with our partner in arms Larry Kudlow, who would soon become Trump's chief economist in the White House, got an urgent call from our longtime friend Corey Lewandowski. Corey was then the Trump campaign manager, and an unsung hero of the Trump political phenomenon. Without Lewandowski's skilled management of the campaign against a minefield of strong Republican challengers—including former Florida governor Jeb Bush, Texas senator Ted Cruz, Kentucky Senator Rand Paul, and Florida senator Marco Rubio, among others (and all of whom we have the highest respect for)—Donald Trump would never have been president.

His message for us would change our lives. "Donald would like to meet the three of you," Corey explained. "Could you meet him at four p.m. next Tuesday at his office in Trump Tower in Manhattan?"

Wow. That was unexpected. When Trump had announced his run for the White House—about six months before—we, like most people, thought it was mostly a publicity stunt. Trump was saying some headline-grabbing things, throwing out a blizzard of populist policy ideas for the American people to chew over: "Build the wall." "Repeal NAFTA." "The biggest tax cut ever." Meanwhile he was drawing massive, excited crowds at his political rallies across the country.

Trump, although politically inexperienced and disdained by the Mediocracy and the professional political class, was connecting with millions of voters.

We were initially skeptical of Trump. He was part of the New York City scene and had never taken on a significant role in the conservative free market movement. His statements on finance seemed to us to be all over the map, a pastiche of conservative and progressive ideas. True, we were iconoclasts ourselves, and some of our own ideas—our advocacy of a more open legal immigration policy and our confidence that economic growth could balance the budget—were considered borderline heretical by some factions of the conservative coalition to which we belonged.

We had written columns critical of several of Trump's positions, especially on trade. We were and are staunch free traders. Larry and Arthur had met Trump on many occasions in the past and liked him very much personally. Steve had never met Trump and was somewhat turned off by his brash, media-hogging style.

But we loved Trump's unyielding optimism about America's potential for an American economic renaissance, which would pull us out of the slow-growth ditch the nation had careened into during George W. Bush's last years in office and Barack Obama's entire presidency. Joe Biden talks about "middle class out" policies, but Trump was advocating policies that would lift the middle class out of its nine-year economic funk.

Trump was proclaiming that we could get to 5 percent growth with the right set of pro-business policy ideas. Though we thought that 5 percent was overly optimistic (we thought 3 to 4 percent was definitely doable), we loved the aspiration! We recognized that Trump, as a real estate developer who built skyscrapers and five-star resorts, thinks very big and does not shy away from dramatic license. The October 6, 2016, issue of The New Yorker (in an obvious attempted character assassination just before the election) reported Trump saying to [architect Der] Scutt, ahead of a 1980 press conference, "Give them the old Trump bull[s*&%]. Tell them it is going to be a million square feet, sixty-eight stories..."

Incidentally, one thing we've learned over the past nine years of getting to know and working with Donald Trump. Yes, he exaggerates.

We certainly agreed—wholeheartedly—that the economy could grow much, much faster than most economists believed. The standard trope on the left at the time was that 1 to 2 percent growth was the best America could achieve. After all, if the left's political messiah, Barack Obama, couldn't get the economy moving faster, how could a mere mortal like Donald Trump presume to?

We were ecstatic that finally someone was frontally assaulting the tyranny of low expectations that sold America short.

And we loved that Trump seemed to relish that the professional political class ridiculed his Make America Great Again (MAGA) theme. We did not agree with all Trump's policy prescriptions. That said, he certainly had all the right enemies attacking him.

So, yes, we told Corey, we definitely wanted to meet with candidate Donald Trump.

TRUMP TOWER

A few days later we arrived at Trump Tower in New York City and sifted through the massive security detail and what seemed like a tsunami of media cameras in the lobby, heading up to the twenty-sixth floor . . . and Donald Trump's personal office.

We won't go into all the details of that meeting that certainly won us over to his side. All of this is covered in our 2017 book *Trumponomics*.

What we remember most about that meeting was Trump sitting behind his giant desk and all six foot four, 220 pounds of him hunched toward us—and asking right out of the gate: "How am I doing?" he asked, as he always did throughout the campaign. He proved inquisitive about everything. "What do you think of my tax plan?" "Is the economy headed to a recession?" "Don't you think we have to worry about China?" "We're doing great in the polls, have you seen our numbers?" (Yes, even back then Trump showed an obsession with the polls.) "What should we do about the deficit?"

One of the first things Steve said to him was: "I just attended one of your rallies a few weeks ago and met a lot of the people there. Donald, I don't know if I love you, but I sure love your voters." Trump almost burst out of his chair. "I love these people too. They're the greatest Americans, aren't they? They love our country." (Now you know why he loved to do political rallies even as president. They recharge his batteries.)

We discussed trade. We discussed taxes. We discussed energy policy. We discussed money and the Fed. We discussed middle class remedies.

Trump knew full well we were on the free trade side, while he publicly and stubbornly declared that he was more for "fair" than "free" trade. A few months earlier Larry and Steve had penned a piece in *National Review* called "Smoot-Hawley-Trump," arguing that Trump could wreck the economy should he follow in the footsteps of Herbert Hoover, the last (and disastrously!) protectionist president. Hoover signed the infamous Smoot-Hawley tariff. That bill exacerbated the Great Depression by inciting a global trade war.

Then he got the point of the meeting: "Will you help me write a tax plan that is even bigger than Reagan's?" We looked at each other, grinned, and said: "We're in."

TRUMP'S STREET-SMART ECONOMICS

That first meeting lasted about 50 minutes.

When we walked out of that meeting, we all simultaneously looked at each other with our jaws dropped. We all had the exact same thought. "My God, he's going to win."

We sensed that he instinctively "gets" what makes an economy work. Why wouldn't he? Unlike Joe Biden and Kamala Harris, who have little to no private-sector experience, Trump has what we call "Street Smarts Economics." Clear away the excessive government taxation, bureaucracy, red tape, and inane rules . . . and much faster growth is possible. Trump knows this not from studying economics books but from his own business background and his many interactions with government agencies in Washington and New York City. Economists and politicians only study and talk about the economy, which is made up of Donald Trump and people a lot like him! It is doers and risk takers like Donald Trump who put our ideas into action. Love him or hate him, Donald Trump has New York street smarts—and that's worth a lot.

This surely injures the vanity of the Ivory Tower snobs. Yet when it comes to getting the job done—creating jobs and economic growth—the voters were starting to show more smarts than the intelligentsia.

And there was something else. The two of us have been around politicians all our working lives. We've met all the presidents since Reagan. Arthur goes back to President Nixon, whom he worked for in the White House under George Shultz. In fact, Arthur has a Camp David windbreaker given to him in 1971 when he was involved in the formulation of Nixon's "New Economic Policy," which included the temporary closing of the gold window.

Trump connects. The only three presidents with whom we've interacted who demonstrated that uncanny ability to connect—to light up a room when they walk in? Ronald Reagan, Bill Clinton, and Barack Obama. And now, Donald Trump.

Trump demonstrated to us that "X factor" so critical to winning elections and succeeding in politics.

It's easy to forget that at the time when Corey called us in, Trump was causing a cardiac arrest within the GOP establishment because he was winning. It was still topsy-turvy, and Trump had suffered setbacks in a few early primaries. He lost Iowa to Texas senator Ted Cruz. The political insiders believed that the odds were still heavily stacked against him winning the primary, let alone the general election.

But we could sense what Trump did. Americans—especially in the Rust Belt states of the Midwest—were fed up with the political elite—of both parties. (Does this sound at all familiar to the attitude of voters today?)

At that time, as now, America had badly underperformed for years. Following the economic and stock market collapse of 2008, voters chased Republicans from office and elected a charismatic politician in Barack Obama—who could have been a hero in rebuilding the American economy.

Instead, it was tax and spend madness and the nation endured eight years of a flatlined middle class. The weak recovery under Obama was deeply disappointing and had flattened middle-class income growth. Average gross domestic product (GDP) growth was tortoise-paced over the past decade and a half. Jobs weren't coming back, except for low-paying menial and unskilled jobs. Obamacare was making healthcare unaffordable. Annual federal deficits were averaging more than $1 trillion. Big business bailouts and welfare handouts were becoming the norm. Republicans should have won back the White House in 2012, but they ran a patrician candidate in Mitt Romney with an uninspiring and tired message that voters rejected.

By 2016 the elites on the left and the right were so out of touch that they were flabbergasted to discover how unhappy Americans were with the state of affairs in America. They were oblivious to their own polls, which had shown for years that about two-thirds of voters believed the country was going in "the wrong direction." Only two candidates in America seemed to recognize and capitalize on this voter unrest: Trump on the right and Bernie Sanders on the left.

As a consequence, the inconceivable happened: Donald J. Trump—with no political experience, and a brash real estate mogul and star of the TV hit show The Apprentice, who was most known by Americans for his memorable line, "You're fired!"—trounced his GOP challengers. Six months later in one of the greatest political upsets in American history, he took out Hillary Clinton—the queen of Washington establishment thinking.

We took a LOT of heat from many of our conservative friends for backing Trump in 2016. Everyone we knew—and we mean everyone—believed that Trump would be a flash in the pan. The polls couldn't possibly be right. Odds makers on betting lines still had his chances of winning the presidency at about 1 in 20. When he announced six months earlier his intention to run for the White House, he was the 100-to-1 underdog. A Hillary operative once told us that it was more likely that the New York Islanders would beat the New York Knicks in basketball than that Trump would ever beat Clinton.

The more outrageous Trump's statements, the more his voters seemed to adore him. As we would soon learn firsthand, with Trump it was always "another day, another banner headline or lead cable news story."

Steve attended a Trump political rally in early 2016, mostly out of curiosity, but it was there that he had an epiphany about Trump. The crowds were large and boisterous—with the energy level of a Rolling Stones concert. But what was shocking was the type of people who attended. This wasn't the country club set.

These were people we now describe as prototypical Trump voters and whom Steve mentioned to Trump in that first meeting—blue-collar, working-class, culturally conservative folks not strongly aligned with either party. They were angry, patriotic, frustrated, financially stressed out, and searching for a great change of direction for a nation that they believed was showing all the symptoms of an economic and cultural breakdown.

There were schoolteachers, cops, construction workers, bikers (hundreds of motorcycles parked on the side of Trump rallies), soccer moms, grandparents, small businessmen and businesswomen. A surprising number of blacks and Hispanics were among this crowd of attendees. When asked what they liked about Trump, they said things like "He speaks his mind about what's wrong with America," "We need someone who will rattle the cages," "He will shake things up in Washington," "The fake news media lies about him," "I'm sick of politicians, we need a successful businessman." These were voters who didn't like Obama at all, but they also had little good to say about George W. Bush.

Neither party was paying attention to these voters, and when either party did pay attention, it was nothing more than a patronizing pat on the head. Many times we felt the same frustration with the political class.

What so many of these voters liked most about Donald Trump was that he would drain the Washington swamp.

The political left ignored and dismissed these voter complaints as irrational and witless—in the end to their own detriment. Hillary Clinton was so contemptuous of this voter uprising that she infamously told a group of her millionaire and billionaire donors that many Trump voters were "deplorables" and, even, "irredeemable." The left regularly ridiculed the Trump voters as xenophobes, Islamophobes, racists, misogynists, and homophobes who wanted to turn back the clock.

The view of most political elites—both Republican and Democratic—was that they were culturally, morally, and intellectually superior to the Trump troops. They had, and showed, contempt for working people.

When we would ask the folks at these rallies or later during the campaign what they thought about the Obama recovery, they would often respond with disdain: "What recovery? This is Michigan." Or Ohio. Or Illinois. Or West Virginia. Or upstate New York. Or Iowa. Or the other half of America—not on the coasts and not connected to Hollywood, Silicon Valley, Wall Street, or Washington, D.C.

The more the left threw temper tantrums over Trump, the more voters he attracted. It turns out he was speaking for tens of millions of what are now called the "forgotten Americans."

He was P. T. Barnum. What a showman! He was funny. His rallies were fun and entertaining. He was saying things that many tens of millions of Americans agreed with but in this era of political correctness and lectures about "hate speech" were afraid to say themselves.

Was there some demagoguery here? Sure. But it always made us laugh that when Trump said "build the wall" he was denounced as a dangerous demagogue, whereas when Barack Obama promised to prevent the rise of the oceans, he was viewed like a Greek god as the media swooned over his stage presence and charisma.

THE TRUMP COMEBACK CIRCA 2024

Okay. Let's come to a full stop here.

Does any of what we just described about the 2016 campaign sound familiar?

Isn't this EXACTLY what we are seeing in 2024? Biden, Kamala, the *New York Times*, AOC, CNN, NPR, and blue state politicians seem indignant and horrified that voters might want him back in office. Many of our Republican friends keep reciting this line to us that Trump is the only one who could lose to Joe Biden. Just as he was "the only one who would lose to Hillary

Clinton." They may be right that he will lose—to Kamala Harris. But we wouldn't bet on it.

TRUMP'S 2024 POLITICAL COMEBACK

So now we fast forward to this current campaign. When we met with Trump at his office in Bedminster, NJ it was like we were starting right where we left off. We sat in the waiting room outside his office overlooking the swimming pool and the first hole of the golf course, and in a short while Trump himself comes bounding out of his office with an enthusiastic smile. Usually in this situation an aide would usher visitors like us into the room to see the President, but it was quite flattering that he would come out and get us. As an aside, one thing we have learned about Trump is that he has this special talent of making everyone he meets feel special and important. We've seen this firsthand so many times. Whether it is a Senator, a governor, a foreign dignitary, a cabinet secretary, a member of his country club, or even the waitress, or the chauffer, or a grandmother at a Trump rally, he displays no arrogance in his personal relationships. He tries to learn something new from everyone he comes across. And nearly everyone is beaming after a meeting with Donald J. Trump.

On this occasion, Trump told us that he had asked us to come because he wanted to in effect put the band back together. After some small talk, including his question of what was his greatest mistake as president? To which we replied unhesitatingly: Not firing Anthony Fauci, the villain of Covid." Trump acknowledged that was a mistake. He wanted us to help him again in 2020 with the rebuilding job ahead. Remember, the primaries had not even begun, let alone the general election fight. We had some doubts at that time about whether he could recreate the magic of 2016, but we learned there was no saying no to Donald Trump. Just as eight years ago, we said: "We're in." Then he added: "Make sure Larry [Kudlow] is in." There was no doubt about that. Kudlow and Trump have a unique bond of trust and mutual admiration. So we signed on to be senior economic advisors.

(For the record: Neither of us have ever been paid by Trump of the campaign in any of his three presidential runs. We have always served as volunteer consultants.)

One priority, we told the President in that early on discussion, was that we needed to sharply compare and contrast the Trump and Biden presidencies on the economy. (See chapter 2 for the full comparison.) Trump has always had a fascination with Ronald Reagan, probably the most popular president of the past half-century. He always peppers Laffer with question about the Gipper as if to ask: "What would Reagan do?"

We told Trump that the similarities between this election and that of the 1980 election when Reagan ran against the incumbent president Jimmy Carter. Then as now, inflation was raging, America's foreign policy was a mess, illegal immigration was out of control, middle-class incomes were falling, gas prices were surging, and it seemed to Americans that the economy and the country were headed over a cliff. We recited to Trump what Reagan had asked 100 million Americans watching the famous debate against Jimmy Carter in 1980: "Are you better off than you were four years ago?" Then, as now, the answer is no.

To buttress this point, we had come to the meeting armed with a chart book that we had put together with the help of our friend and Trump confidante Lee Rizzuto. The chart book compared Trump and Biden on about 30 different metrics on the economy. We walked him through the flip chart. On virtually every one of these kitchen table measurements of middle-class well-being, Trump far outperformed Biden. This included everything from take-home pay, to inflation, to gas prices, to mortgage interest rates, to 401k plan returns, to minority poverty rates, to grocery bills, to credit card debts, to domestic energy production, to stock market performance after adjusting for inflation, and so on. This chart book has gone viral and has become a hallmark of the economic case for Trump in 30 pictures and graphs.

At one point Trump looked at the title we put on the booklet. Our working title was "The Trump Boom and the Biden Bust." Trump thought about it, and then suggested: "I think we should call it 'The Greatest Economic Boom Ever.' Don't you." We fidgeted a little and felt a little uneasy about this because there probably were booms even more impressive than this one. But Trump was clearly over the moon about this report. He was so ebullient that he ushered us downstairs to a meeting of the Trump campaign team. Sitting around a large conference room table were assembled the campaign brain trust troika of Jason Miller, Susi Wiles, and Chris La Civita, plus about 10 or 12 other deputies.

Trump picked up the chartbook and started flipping through it showing the pictures to his team with bubbly enthusiasm. "Use these whenever possible," he instructed the team.

We should add here that our view is that this has been a spectacularly run campaign as we run down the stretch. The Miller, Wiles, and LaCivita team has punched all the right buttons and has been nearly flawless in its election year strategy. One of the other stars who we have worked with is Vince Haley, who has been the chief speechwriter and policy director for Trump on this 2024 campaign. He has performed brilliantly. So have Brooke Rollins and Linda McMahon—who lead the America First Policy Institute and have provided sage policy advice to team Trump. They are putting together a team of extraordinarily talented people to run the agencies of government when Trump gets back in the White House.

As with any great CEO, Trump surrounds himself with immensely talented people.

We've often conceded to those who dislike Trump that there is a "good Trump and a bad Trump." We saw too much of the bad Trump during the 2020 campaign in its aftermath culminating in the violence at the Capital on January 6th. What has impressed us most in our periodic interactions with Trump over the past nine months has been his positivity, his clarity of vision on where he wants to lead the country, and his contagious belief that America can quickly get back on track. This is the "good Trump."

When we asked him about how long it would take to resurrect the economy, he replied: "Give me six months." That's a flash in time given that it has taken Biden just under four years to ruin the economy and put us $6 trillion further into debt. His strategy, he told us, was to "have a stack of papers on my desk in the Oval Office on January 22nd, each one an executive order repealing much of the Biden agenda." That too was music to our ears.

As we left that meeting Steve mentioned on the way out that we knew he could make the American economy great again, because he already had done it once. "No, actually, Steve," he replied, "I did it twice. I did it after Obama. And I did it after Covid."

We stood corrected.

The rest of this book is the story of "The Trump Economic Miracle"—or should we say MIRACLES?—and the agenda that will make America great again, again.

CHAPTER 1

How Trump Saved the American Economy

"America is open for business, and we are competitive once again."

"The world is witnessing the resurgence of a strong and prosperous America.... There has never been a better time to hire, to build, to invest, and to grow in the United States."

—Donald Trump at Davos, 2018

At the start of the Trump presidency, the two of us wrote *Trumponomics: Inside the America First Plan to Save Our Economy.*

Trump did save the economy. He did regain American prosperity in what was one of the greatest economic miracles in modern history. When we told him in early 2024 that we were writing this book, Trump—with his usually modesty—told us to be sure to call it "the greatest economic recovery EVER." That's a Trumpian exaggeration, but not much of one. Americans sure saw a boost of economic confidence when Trump took over from Obama, and then when he left office, Americans' outlook on the economy plummeted as Biden-Harris policies took hold.

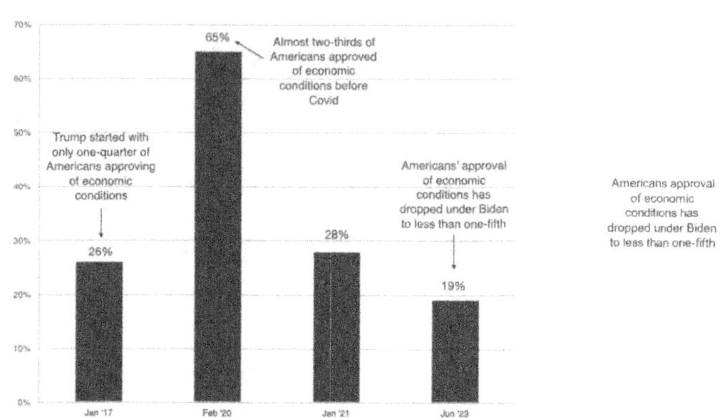

After all, middle-class family incomes rose by $6,000 after inflation—the most in a president's four-year term. The poverty and unemployment rates dropped for nearly every demographic group, including blacks and Hispanics, to all-time lows.

All-Time Low Unemployment for Minorities under Trump

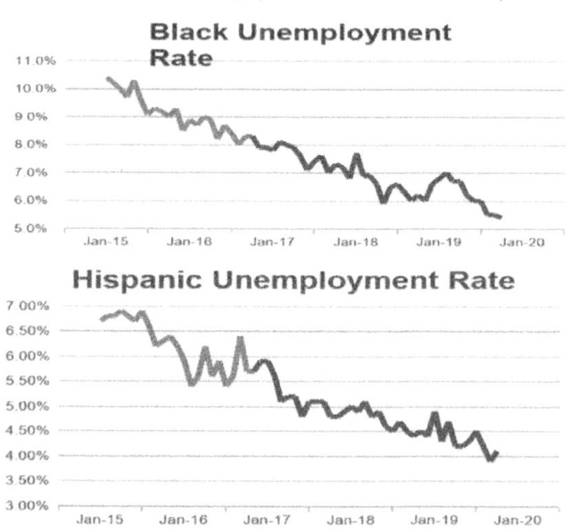

The Trump Economic Miracle

The left talks a lot about a "great reset on the American economy." There has been a great reset and it was Trump's Make America Great Again agenda. But Biden and Harris have in less than four years reversed course and driven the American economy into a debt-drenched ditch.

So here we are some six years after the publication of *Trumponomics* and the American economy needs saving again, with a healthy dose of anabolic steroids.

Every four years, politicians and pundits say, "This is the most important election in our lifetime." We don't care for that platitude, but it's safe to say that it's a pretty damn important election. And when it comes to the economy, the two candidates are orbits apart. Trump is on Venus and Biden is on Mars.

Four years ago we thought and prayed that Biden would govern from the middle, the way another recent Democrat, Bill Clinton, did so successfully. Remember, Biden campaigned on being a "uniter." The *New York Times* joyously proclaimed in big bold headlines: "Now It Is Time to Unite." These same voices were never in favor of uniting when Trump was president. Hillary declared the day after she lost that Democrats should be the "resistance"—and she said this even before he entered office and put in place his plan. Gee, that was unifying.

But far from being a uniter, Biden divided the country down the middle with an extremely left-wing tax, spend and regulate agenda that almost no one expected—certainly not millions of those who voted for him. You don't have to take our word for that. Bernie Sanders, AOC, and all the liberal members of the radical House Democrat "Squad" have praised Biden's "progressive" policies as a dream come true.

The Democratic narrative—often repeated by Kamala Harris —is that Biden rescued the economy from Covid. That's a rewrite of history. The economy was on the mend when Biden came into office, having snapped back to life from Covid lockdowns. Economic growth was a stunning 11% in the last six months Trump was in office. That's one of the fastest recoveries EVER. The new life-saving vaccine was widely distributed thanks to Operation Warp Speed, and businesses were opening their doors again—alas, much faster in red states than in blue states.

We would argue the stakes are even higher in the 2024 election than the 2016 election, when Trump defeated Hillary Clinton. We shudder when we look at the avalanche of destructive policies that have come out of this administration and that have been endorsed by the Kamala Harris campaign– including a war on American energy, the highest inflation rates since the era of Jimmy Carter, gas prices up 40%, a leaky southern border with at least eight million new illegal immigrants let in, the implosion of our inner cities, declining home ownership, the weakling response to events around the world (such as the catastrophic tail-between-our-legs exit from Afghanistan), the decline of American power around the world, the regulatory explosion, the move to ban everything from air conditioners to gas-powered SUVs, and a national debt that has risen by some $6 trillion over three years. Obama's economic record was rather dismal on most measures of economic progress, but Biden's has been worse—*much* worse—and far more liberal.

We find it ironic that many Wall Street and academic economists have declared that Kamala and the Democrats would be better at controlling inflation and the debt than Trump. But when we put Biden's record on each of these records side-by-side against Trump's we see the opposite result. To borrow a line often attributed to Groucho Marx, "who you gonna believe, me, or your own two eyes."

Trump Versus Biden on Inflation, Interest Rates and Debt

	Trump	Biden
Cumulative Inflation	8%	19.5%
Annual Inflation	2%	6%
Mortgage Interest Rate	3%	7%
Ten Year Treasury	1%	4.5%
Annual Deficits* (billions)	$750	$1,500

*Excludes Covid years of 2020 and 2021.

But the story gets worse because unlike in 2020 when Biden ran as a centrist Democrat, this time around Kamala isn't even pretending that she will govern from the middle. In her entire Senate career, the only bills of hers that passed had no Republican cosponsors. She is nothing if not a fierce partisan.

She's promised to double-down on a Che Guevera-type agenda that would bring the "great transition" to big government socialism the left has so often longed for. We now have a Democratic ticket that pairs the Senator who scored the most liberal voting record in congress, with Tim Walz of Minnesota, one of the three most liberal governors in America. We don't know precisely where that will lead us, but we know the destination won't be prosperity.

Kamala has embraced Bidenomics, and Bidenomics 2.0, which includes the biggest tax rate increases since the 1930s. She's proposed another $2 trillion of spending on programs Biden didn't get through in his first term—because apparently $6 trillion of added programs wasn't enough. She has adopted the Biden tax plan to tax unrealized capital gains for the first time, so that people would literally have to sell the farm to pay the taxes. She and the Senate Democrats would likely end the filibuster, so it would take only 51 votes, not 60, to pass their radical agenda. There would be a move to pack the Supreme Court with 2, 4, or 6 new justices, so the left would have a blank check from the courts to run roughshod over constitutional restraints (even FDR at the peak of his popularity was not able to pull that off). There would be a move to end the Electoral College, to change the voting rules permanently, and to make Puerto Rico and Washington, DC states, so the Democrats would have four more Senate seats. The two moderate voices in the Senate—Kyrsten Sinema of Arizona and Joe Manchin of West Virginia—who heroically saved the filibuster and stifled other power grabs by Biden, will be gone from the Senate after 2024.

The radical climate change agenda would have a full speed ahead mandate from voters. Gas cars and gas stoves and plastic bags would be outlawed. Rationing of electricity could be coming and so could blackouts and brownouts. Just look at what has happened in California in recent years.

In fact, we have often made the case that Kamala Harris, as a died-in-the-wool San Francisco progressive Democrat wants to remake the U.S. economy in the image of the California economy. This is a scary proposition since the Golden State is now a disaster, with a declining population, out of control regulation, far-left cultural mandates, and persistently high levels of debt.

Readers may think we are engaging in histrionics here, but all of these ideas have been openly floated by Kamala Harris at one time or another—although she has sprinted away from her record since becoming the Democrats' nominee for President. We can forgive Americans if they are confused. As the Wall Street Journal put it: "Will the real Kamala Harris please stand up?" The woman is a political chameleon, who changes colors and positions depending on who she is talking to.

There is one other key difference between Trump and Kamala that explains a lot about how they could look at the same country and come up with diametrically opposite policy conclusions. Kamala—like Biden—is a lifelong politician. She has seldom if ever earned a paycheck from a private business and she certainly has never run a business. Maybe this explains her dismal record in running operations, such as when she was named border czar and instead of securing the border, she oversaw the worst border crisis in history.

Trump, by contrast, has spent virtually his entire career building businesses, employing people, battling against intrusive and often mindless bureaucratic regulations. He knows how to create jobs, make a payroll, earn a profit. Kamala is like a nine-year old behind the wheel of a Porsche speeding down the highway with no knowledge of how to drive. It's not going to end well, just as Bidenomics hasn't.

THE REAL DONALD TRUMP

Which brings us back to Trump—the man who we have had the privilege of informally advising for the past decade. Donald Trump is not the person the media has so unfairly portrayed. He is certainly not the villain, conniving and intellectually shallow man that his adversaries have portrayed him as since the day he first announced he was running for president back in 2015.

Is Donald Trump crazy, we are often asked? Yes, crazy like a fox.

Does he have personality flaws? Absolutely. Does he love the adulation? Absolutely.

So did Reagan. So did Clinton. So did Obama. So did JFK.

Is he sometimes his own worst enemy? Yes.

This book is not meant to be a celebration of Trump. Every American by now has clearly made up his own mind about Trump's larger-than-life personality. We clearly have an admiration for the man and consider him a friend. Trump awarded one of us (Laffer) the Presidential Medal of Freedom. But more importantly, most of his policy goals are in line with our own, which is why we signed on to help him as informal advisers. (Neither of us have ever been on his campaign payroll in 2016, 2020, or 2024.)

And we wouldn't be helping him today if we thought he was deranged, dangerous, delusional, or unfit for office as so many liberals seem to insist think of him. We wouldn't have agreed to work for him if we thought his economic ideas were destructive, simple-minded or inconsistent with what has become known as "the Kudlow Creed"—"free market capitalism is the best path to prosperity." (Even Trump has used that phraseology when we have met with him.)

So we have a bias in describing Trump in part because we like him, we believe in him, and we think he can recreate the economic magic that he unleashed in his first term. When we met with him recently at Mar-a-Lago, we told him we were sure that he could rebuild the economy because he already did it once. Without skipping a beat, he instantly corrected us: "I rebuilt the economy TWICE," he thundered. "First when we rebuilt from the mess we were handed from Obama and then after Covid." He's right about that.

Trump has a pro-growth economic agenda that really can "Make America Great Again…Again"—and this book aims to explain how. But we also want to present the good, the bad, and the ugly of Trump.

We are free traders and have flinched at some of Trump's more protectionist instincts. On several occasions, we tried to temper some of his more ill-conceived trade ideas, such as repealing NAFTA, which has made the economy more dynamic and more competitive. Sometimes (but not always) we succeeded in reining in his trade policy. On immigration, we agreed with many of Trump's restrictions that are based on national security and anti-terrorism priorities. Keeping undesirables out of our country is one of the first responsibilities of a sovereign nation dedicated to protecting its citizens. But, of course, we are in favor of legal immigration and always told Trump, if you build that wall, make sure it has big gates as well.

In 2016, when Trump pulled off the upset of the century, there was hatred of Trump and everything he stood for. Liberals used to argue with some grains of truth that conservatives were knee-jerk in opposing everything Barack Obama tried to do, even when he occasionally had good ideas. But the left should look in the mirror.

Amazingly, we can only count on one hand the few times when Biden has had a good idea. He did put out an executive order to try to pull back on occupational licensing rules that restrict competition in industries.

Trump has adroitly argued to his tens of millions of steadfast supporters that when the elite attack him and his policies, and recklessly use the police powers of government against him (remember the Russia collusion hoax that almost led to Trump's impeachment), they are coming after not just him, but his voters.

He's right. Even some of Trump's economic advisers have gone to jail or have been convicted for the crime of supporting Trump and keeping their private conversations with the president private. Sometimes we worry that the FBI will be knocking on our doors if Trump loses.

At the start of 2024, the "never Trump" elites assured us there was no way that there were enough Trump voters for him to again win the 2024 Republican nomination. They were wrong again. He blew away a strong field including Nikki Haley, Florida governor Ron DeSantis, former Vice President Mike Pence, and Senator Tim Scott. Now they can't imagine that there are 51% of Americans who might vote him back into office.

We will pause here to note that we are often asked what Trump and Ronald Reagan have in common. We have always said three things: First, they loved people. Second, they loved America as a "shining city on a hill" and a "beacon of freedom"—and emphasized the country's greatness. And third, they were ALWAYS underestimated by their political opponents.

Instead of trying to figure out how it is that Trump has captured such a large share of the middle class and working-class Americans who were traditionally Democratic, the Trump haters (on the left and the right) thumb their noses at the Trump voters. They have come to believe that they are culturally, morally, and intellectually superior to blue-collar America. They STILL believe that the Trump voters are deplorables.

But in most cases their economic ideas are not superior to Trump's. As this book shows in the chapters to come, we've had a clash of economic visions over the last seven years. On most of the official economic measures—on incomes, inflation, gas prices, deficits, border security, interest rates, homeownership, and others—Trump's record is superior.

One of our points of emphasis in this book is that we long for the day when Democrats were a pro-growth, pro-tax cutting party. Our good friend and colleague, Larry Kudlow, wrote a book in 2016 entitled *JFK and the Reagan Revolution*, which points out that not only have tax cuts been highly associated with prosperity and "a rising tide that lifts all boats," but it was the DEMOCRATS of the 1960s who were behind these pro-growth policies (and the Eisenhower and Goldwater Republicans who were against them). But for several decades now, the Democrats have been steadfast in their opposition to tax cutting. Hillary Clinton and Bernie Sanders ran on raising tax rates to 50 percent or more. We long for a return of the JFK Democrats.

WHAT IS TRUMPONOMICS?

We wish we had some bitcoins for every time we have been asked this question over the last eight years. So many people—especially in the media—don't get it. They attack something they don't understand.

The short answer is that every decision Trump makes is about putting America first. And whether you liked Trump's policies in his first term or not—and we think they were for the most part a smashing success—nearly every decision was based on a judgment of whether the policy would advance or retard America's economic and national security interests. That said, we haven't always agreed with Trump's decisions—especially when it came to Covid lockdowns and spending programs, which we believe were driven by a panic mentality that gripped Washington in those early months of 2020.

Trump knows when we disagree with him—but to his credit he still values and solicits our advice and input. We respect that Trump doesn't surround himself with "yes" men. His first-term economic team of Steven Mnuchin, Russ Vought, Larry Kudlow, Kevin Hassett, Linda McMahon, Tyler Goodspeed, Casey Mulligan, Bob Lighthizer, Brooke Rollins and many others was top notch. We're convinced he will have a stellar crowd around him in his second term. That list is likely to include smart and effective leaders including Scott Bessent of Key Square, Jamie Dimon of J.P. Morgan, Lee Rizzuto, Chris Wright of Liberty Energy, former OMB director Russ Vought, former Federal Reserve governor Kevin Warsh, former Council of Economic Advisers chair Kevin Hassett, former North Dakota governor Dough Burgum, Larry Kudlow (if he can be pried away from Fox), and many other talented people.

The two of us served mostly as outside counsel to Trump while he was in the White House and served on several of his economic task forces in informal roles. But we met with him often, and of course Trump awarded one of us (Laffer) the Presidential Medal of Freedom. When we would visit with him in the Oval Office every several months, he would beam and say, "two of the most brilliant economists." We can't say for sure whether he says that to all the advisers he meets with! But he does have an endearing way of making everyone he meets feel special.

Truth be told, many times when we've disagreed with his decisions, he's proven us wrong, as with his ability to use tariffs as a tool to advance American objectives.

As for his ideas, they are far from orthodox Republican. He is not a captive of the balanced budget obsession, thank God. His top priority is economic growth and job creation. And he also gets something that almost no Democrat and too few Republicans get. No matter how sharp the spending ax, the budget will never be balanced without robust growth in jobs and output. You want more taxes: get wages up and unemployment rates down.

When we would advise Trump that his tax cut, deregulation, and pro-America energy policies could get America back to 3 or 4 percent growth, he would often interrupt us and say, "I want 5 percent growth." This is a guy who shoots for the stars and why not? When Kennedy said he was going to put a man on the moon by the end of the 1960s, many scoffed and said it was technically impossible and fiscally unaffordable, but it happened (in July 1969). Trump faces these "limits to growth" skeptics every day.

One of our favorite moments on the campaign was when the liberals in the media complained that he would not be able to build a wall. They practically shouted in unison, "He can't do it and he doesn't know how to do." Trump replied: "I've built skyscraper buildings all over the world. How hard can it be to build a wall?" And most Americans agreed with him.

TRUMP'S ECONOMIC PHILOSOPHY

Donald Trump is NOT an ideological conservative. Reagan was far more schooled in conservative thought and was more dedicated to the principles of limited government. Trump is for common sense. He is a populist in many ways—for better or for worse. In most cases, the people are right and the elites in government are wrong. We were struck by a recent comment from the onetime Federal Reserve Chairman, Janet Yellen. She was criticizing a view held by many conservative economists and by Trump that monetary policy should be dictated by rules, not by the discretion of a few "wise men and women" who sit on the Federal Reserve Board and act as if they can steer the economy through interest rate policies. She was dead wrong and that thinking helped push the economy over the cliff in 2008-09 and led to a very shallow recovery in the Obama years.

Is Trump a Keynesian on spending policy? He wants to spend $1 trillion more on infrastructure and hundreds of billions more on the military. We have warned him that "shovel ready projects" and trillions of dollars of borrowing under Obama failed to revive the American economy and very likely retarded the rebound rather than enhanced it. We also cringe at the idea of more questionable infrastructure projects (like the infamous "bridge to nowhere" in Alaska) or more bullet trains to nowhere in California. But there will be economic benefits if Trump can rebuild our energy infrastructure—pipelines, LNG terminals, refineries (not with federal but private dollars)—and if he can modernize our shipping ports, our electric grid system, and airports, and if he can leverage private dollars to pay for roads and bridges to end traffic delays.

But the infrastructure development America needs today is in the private sector. We need more factories, more business startups, more warehouses and laboratories, and more trucks and forklifts and robots and modern factories so America can once again be a hub of innovation and manufacturing. The naysayers who say that jobs in manufacturing, in coal, and in other traditionally blue-collar sectors are gone for good don't realize the power of incentive economics. The sickness in the economy over the last decade has been the sharp decline in business investment. This investment is the seed corn of a growing economy.

Sometimes we are asked to identify the best thing about Trump and Trumponomics? The answer is simple: "it worked." And the best thing about returning to Trump policies, "Trumponomics 2.0" as some people call it, is that it will mean that the war on business is over. Obama—and more so the people he put in federal agencies—were violently anti-business. But Biden's team has been worse. The Biden White House views business as adversaries and the men and women who run our large American corporations and our 30 million small businesses as enemies of consumers, workers, and the environment. That's not a pro-growth position.

We are not making the case that the people who run businesses are angels (they certainly are not), and we aren't saying we don't need guardrails to protect worker and consumer safety. We are only saying that the economy can't grow and wages can't rise if you don't have healthy businesses. As our old friend Dick Armey used to say, "Liberals love jobs but they hate employers." That may be an exaggeration, but not much of one.

THE KAMALA ELITES VERSUS THE TRUMP WORKING CLASS "DEPLORABLES"

Ever since Hillary Clinton disparaged Trump and his middle-class voter base as "deplorables" in the 2016 campaign, it has been clear that the liberal elites in both parties have never fully understood Trump and his Make America Great Again populist movement. The elites are clearly contemptuous of the intellect and lifestyles of the Trump loyalists.

Liberals should go back and read Jude Wanniski's classic *The Way the World Works*. Wanniski reminds us over and over again of the lesson of history: there is great collective wisdom in the decisions made by the American voters. It's risky to second-guess them; it's much safer to listen to what they are saying.

Today, it's clear that there is a new Republican working class party, and it's positioned against the leftist elites. In 2020, Trump won virtually all of the middle- and working-class counties across the country. He lost the districts of the very poor and the very affluent. This is because Trump is a wrecking ball to the elite vision of America. This cover of *Time* magazine summarized this contempt of the elites in the Washington, DC establishment and the intellectuals in college faculty lounges. Trump the disruptor is what they loath. How dare he dismantle fat, arrogant, expensive and out-of-touch government. But this was what the voters voted FOR. This was all about "draining the swamp."

In early 2024, our group, Unleash Prosperity, commissioned a poll comparing the attitudes of regular Main Street Americans versus what we call the over-educated cultural elite. These are those in the top income strata, who attended Ivy League colleges, who live in urban areas, and hold advanced degrees. The poll results confirmed how out of touch the elite are with working class Americans—most of whom are the Trump voter base.

Here are some prominent examples of how out of touch the elites are from other Americans:

- Personal Financial Situation. Only about 25% of all Americans say they are better off financially today than in the past. But among the elite that number triples to 74% who say they are better off. And among graduates of Ivy League colleges, 78% say they are better off. This may explain the mystery of why the media, academics and high-income Americans tend to rate the economy is good, at the same time that most Americans say the economy is bad.

- Individual Freedom. When Americans are asked if there is too much or too little freedom, elites are three times more likely to say that there is too much individual freedom in America than are all Americans. Almost six of ten of the graduates from elite colleges think there is too much freedom.
- Rationing of Food and Energy to Fight Climate Change. Climate change is clearly an obsession of the very rich and highly educated. An astonishing 67% of the elites, including nearly 80% of the elites who graduated from the top universities, favor rationing of energy, gas, and meat to combat climate change. Among all Americans, 67% oppose this policy.
- Banning Cars and Household Appliances. Between half and two thirds of elites would favor a BAN on a list of modern conveniences, including gas stoves, gas-powered cars, air conditioning, SUVs, and "nonessential air travel" (that would mean no relaxing vacations flights to Hawaii, Bermuda, or Miami Beach). More than two-thirds of Ivy League college grads would ban each of these. For the average Americans, only between 16% and 24% favor any of these bans.

- Approval of Biden as President. At a time when President Biden's approval rating among voters was in the low-40's, his performance earned approval from 84% of the elite 1%.[1]
- Favorable Opinion of the Members of the Talking Professions—Lawyers, lobbyists, Politicians and Journalists. Only about half of Americans have a favorable opinion of lawyers, lobbyists, or union leaders. But almost 80% of the elites have a favorable opinion of this group of professionals and almost 90% of the elite college attendees do. And while only 28% of Americans have a favorable opinion of members of Congress, 67% of elites do.

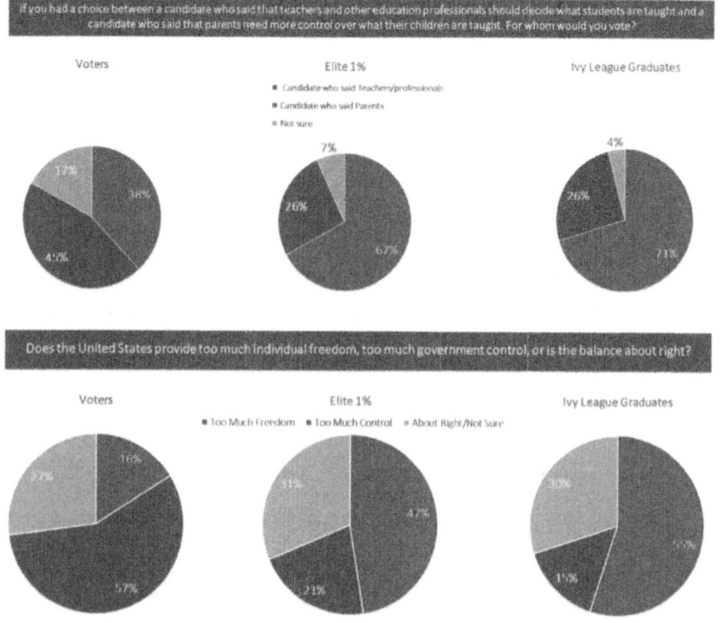

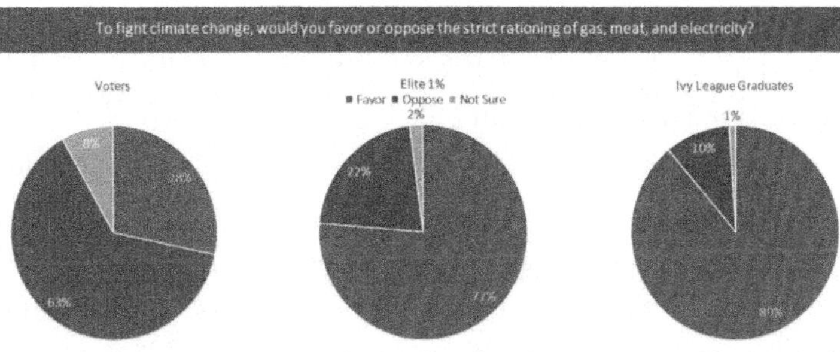

These polling results go a long way in explaining the Trump phenomenon. Wealthy and highly educated elites seem to almost live in a different country than all other Americans. The elites aren't just richer, they put much more trust in big government "to do the right thing." By their own admission, they have benefited far more from the expansive government policies and have been hurt much less by the high inflation of the Biden presidency than those who live from paycheck to paycheck and are in the lower and middle classes.

This Grand Canyon-sized chasm between where everyday Americans stand on the state of the country, expanding government power, and draconian climate change solutions, and Joe Biden's job performance, may partly explain the Donald Trump phenomenon and his high approval ratings among working-class voters. Most of them feel a deep connection to the rebellion against the arrogance of the ruling class elites that Trump personifies.

TRUMP'S ENCORE

Donald Trump's 2016 election was the ultimate "black swan" event, in that it was seen as having a very low probability of happening. But it did happen because he promised the American people a transformative change in U.S. economic policy after eight years of Obama failures. After four years of Biden's lurch toward tax and spend socialist policies, America clearly needs a transformative change again.

Trump won in 2016 by focusing on jobs and the economy—and dismantling the conventional left or right economic agenda. He harnessed a new economic populism that mixed some conventional Republican ideas—tax cuts, deregulation, border security, crime control, and more power to the states—with more traditional Democratic issues—trade protectionism and infrastructure spending. He also ran on a new patriotism, a love of country that has been missing from today's modern Democratic party. Trumpism is about "putting America first," while Bidenism is about "blaming America first."

His outside-the-box political strategy worked like a charm, enabling him to crash through the "Blue Wall" of industrial states like Michigan, Ohio, Pennsylvania, Wisconsin, and Iowa. His populist message strongly resonated with disaffected working-class Americans in these blue-collar states and districts that care about kitchen-table issues like good schools, a growing paycheck, a secure America, and the welfare of their kids, not climate change, transgenderism, and racial quotas.

Trump has proven to be the miracle man when it comes to restoring America's prosperity. This chart below reflects some of the evidence we bring to bear on the superiority of the Trump economic record—especially when we look at progress for women and minorities.

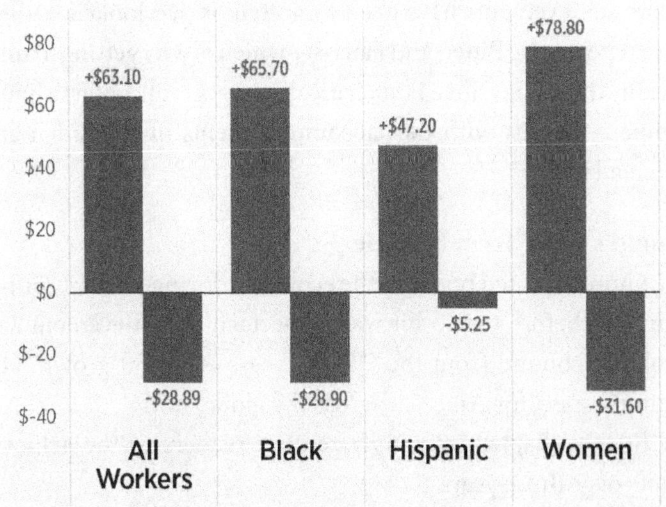

This book is about how he did it in his first, and how he will do it again.

To quote Al Michaels when the last seconds were ticking off during the incredible American victory against the Soviet Union in hockey: "Do you believe in miracles?"

We do. And we believe millions and millions of Americans do as well, which will propel Donald Trump back into the White House.

MIRACLE MAN

This entire book is about Trump's economic triumphs for America. We present a short, but impressive list below. Some of these policy achievements have been forgotten or overlooked, Others were repealed by Biden and Harris—which is why getting Trump back in the Oval Office is so critically important. Voters should compare this list with the "accomplishments of Joe Biden and Kamala Harris.

Trump's First Term Miracle

The unprecedented boom in the economy during the first Trump term and before Covid hit was a spectacular achievement and a robust rebound from the Obama years of pitiful growth and sliding respect for America across the globe.

In this chapter we simply remind readers of the achievements over those years:

ECONOMIC BENEFITS FOR ALL

1) Jobs, Jobs, Jobs. America gained 7 million new jobs—all in the private sector.
2) Surging Incomes for the Middle Class. Middle-class family income increased their real take home incomes by nearly $6,000—more than five times the gains during the entire previous administration.
3) Low Unemployment Rate—The unemployment rate fell to 3.5 percent, the lowest in a half-century. Jobless claims hit a nearly 50-year low.

4) Record Number of Americans Working—Nearly 160 million Americans held jobs during the Biden presidency an all-time record.

RECORD GAINS FOR MINORITIES AND WOMEN

5) Unemployment rates for African Americans, Hispanic Americans, Asian Americans, Native Americans, veterans, individuals with disabilities, and those without a high school diploma all reached record lows
6) Unemployment for women hit its lowest rate in nearly 70 years
7) Poverty rates for African Americans and Hispanic Americans reached record lows
8) Income Inequality and the Racial Income Gap Declined
9) African American homeownership increased to an all-time high

RECORD WEALTH GAINS

10) The DOW closed above 20,000 for the first time in 2017 and topped 30,000 in 2020
11) The S&P 500 and NASDAQ repeatedly notched record highs
12) Trillions of dollars of wealth created for ALL Americans
13) The bottom 50 percent of American households saw a 40 percent increase in net worth.
14) Created more than 1.2 million manufacturing and construction jobs for blue collar workers.

LOWER TAX RATES

15) **Passed $3.2 trillion in historic tax relief and reformed the tax code.**
16) More than 6 million American workers received wage increases, bonuses, and increased benefits thanks to the tax cuts.
17) A typical family of four earning $75,000 received an income tax cut of more than $2,000—slashing their tax bill in half.
18) Doubled the standard deduction to $25,000—now tens of millions of Americans don't have to itemize deductions
19) Eliminated the unfair Estate Tax, or Death Tax for millions of Americans.
20) Cut the business tax rate from 35 percent—the highest in the developed world—all the way down to 21 percent.
21) Small businesses can now deduct 20 percent of their business income—lowering their tax rate to 32% from 40%
22) Businesses can now deduct 100 percent of the cost of their capital investments in the year the investment is made.
23) Over $1.5 trillion was repatriated into the United States from overseas.

HELPED REVITALIZE AMERICAN CITIES JOBS AND INVESTMENTS ARE POURING INTO OPPORTUNITY ZONES.

24) Created nearly 9,000 Opportunity Zones where capital gains on long-term investments are taxed at zero.

25) Opportunity Zones have attracted $75 billion in funds and driven $52 billion of new investment in economically distressed communities, creating at least 500,000 new jobs.

DEREGULATOR IN CHIEF

26) Instead of 2 deregulations for every one new rule, Trump eliminated 4 old regulations for every new regulation adopted.
27) Provided the average American household an extra $3,100 every year.
28) Removed nearly 25,000 pages from the Federal Register—more than any other president. The previous administration added over 16,000 pages.

AMERICAN ENERGY INDEPENDENCE/DOMINATION

29) For the first time in nearly 70 years, the United States has become a net energy exporter.
30) The United States became the number one producer of oil and natural gas in the world.
31) Natural gas production reached a record-high 35 quadrillion BTU.
32) Withdrew U.S. from the anti-America Paris Climate Accord
33) Withdrew from the unfair, one-sided Paris Climate Agreement.
34) Approved the Keystone XL and Dakota Access pipelines. Biden reversed these actions.
35) Opened up the Arctic National Wildlife Refuge (ANWR) in Alaska to oil and gas leasing.

36) Increased LNG exports five-fold since January 2017, reaching an all-time high in January 2020.
37) Re-opened coal production in the U.S. to mine the nations' 600 years of coal reserves.

LOWEST INTEREST RATES AND INFLATION IN MODERN TIMES

38) Inflation under Trump averaged slightly less than 2% per year—below the Federal Reserve target rate
39) Gas Prices fell to below $2 a gallon
40) Mortgage interest rate fell below 3% the lowest in modern times
41) Left office with inflation at 1.5%
42) Interest rates on government bonds lowest in decades

BEST ENVIRONMENTAL RECORD EVER

43) Achieved lowest levels of air pollution in sixty years with 7% reduction
44) Achieved the largest reduction in CO2 emissions in American history
45) Lowered particulate pollution to five times lower than the global average
46) Restored public access to many federal monuments

LIFE-SAVING RESPONSE TO THE CHINA VIRUS

47) Suspended all travel from China, saving thousands of lives
48) Halted American funding to the World Health Organization to counter its egregious bias towards China that jeopardized the safety of Americans.

49) Launched Operation Warp Speed to initiate an unprecedented drive to develop and make available an effective vaccine by January 2021.
50) Pfizer and Moderna developed two vaccines in just nine months, five times faster than the fastest prior vaccine development in American history.
51) Quickly established guidelines for nursing homes and expanded telehealth opportunities to protect vulnerable seniors.

EXPANDED HEALTH CARE CHOICE AND TRANSPARENCY

52) Eliminated the Obamacare individual mandate—a financial relief to low and middle-income households that made up nearly 80 percent of the families who paid the penalty for not wanting to purchase health insurance.
53) Increased choice for consumers by promoting competition in the individual health insurance market leading to lower premiums for three years in a row.
54) Offered Association Health Plans, which allow employers to pool together and offer more affordable, quality health coverage to their employees at up to 30 percent lower cost.
55) Eliminated costly Obamacare taxes, the medical device tax, and the "Cadillac tax."
56) Passed Right to Try Legislation allowing patients—particularly the terminally ill—to try new drugs and treatments.

A FEDERAL JUDICIARY THAT UPHOLDS THE CONSTITUTION

57) Nominated and confirmed over 230 Federal judges.
58) Appointed Justice Neil Gorsuch to replace Justice Antonin Scalia.
59) Appointed Justice Brett Kavanaugh to replace Justice Anthony Kennedy.
60) Appointed Justice Amy Coney Barrett to replace Justice Ruth Bader Ginsburg.

SECURED THE SOUTHERN BORDER OF THE UNITED STATES

61) Built over 400 miles of the world's most robust and advanced border wall.
62) Deployed nearly 5,000 troops to the Southern border. In addition, Mexico deployed tens of thousands of their own soldiers and national guardsmen to secure their side of the US-Mexico border.
63) Ended the dangerous practice of Catch-and-Release, which means that instead of aliens getting released into the United States pending future hearings never to be seen again, they are detained pending removal, and then ultimately returned to their home countries.
64) Signed an executive order to strip discretionary Federal grant funding from deadly sanctuary cities.
65) Fully enforced and implemented statutorily authorized "expedited removal" of illegal aliens.
66) Issued a comprehensive "public charge" regulation to ensure newcomers to the United States are financially self-sufficient and not reliant on welfare.
67) Secured a $400 billion increase in defense spending from NATO (North Atlantic Treaty Organization) allies

by 2024, and the number of members meeting their minimum obligations more than doubled.

68) In 2019, America achieved the largest decline in carbon emissions of any country on earth. Since withdrawing from the Paris Climate Accord, the United States has reduced carbon emissions more than any nation.
69) Between 2017 and 2019, the air became 7 percent cleaner—indicated by a steep drop in the combined emissions of criteria pollutants.
70) Led the world in greenhouse gas emissions reductions, having cut energy-related CO2 emissions by 12 percent from 2005 to 2018 while the rest of the world increased emissions by 24 percent.

CRIMINAL JUSTICE REFORM

71) Passed the most comprehensive criminal justice reform measure The First Step Act in history.
72) Provided training and education and job opportunities to help former inmates successfully rejoin society.

EXPANDING EDUCATIONAL OPPORTUNITY

73) Expanded School Choice, allowing parents to use up to $10,000 from a 529 education savings account to cover K-12 tuition costs at the public, private, or religious school of their choice.
74) Launched a new pro-American lesson plan for students called the 1776 Commission to promote patriotic education.

75) Signed legislation reauthorizing the D.C. Opportunity Scholarship program.

We know there were many more achievements that we have not even mentioned and some that we have forgotten about (and surely Trump will remind us the next time we see him!)

But what is undeniable is that Trump has proven to be the miracle man when it comes to restoring America's prosperity. This book is about how he did it in his first, and how he will do it again.

To quote Al Michaels when the last seconds were ticking off during the incredible American victory against the Soviet Union in hockey: "Do you believe in miracles?"

We do. And we believe millions and millions of Americans do as well, which will propel Donald Trump back into the White House.

CHAPTER 2

From Trump Boom to Bidenomics Bust

When Americans go to the voting booth in November, they will be asking themselves two simple questions: Am I better off than I was four years ago? And is our country better off than it was four years ago? These were the questions that Ronald Reagan, staring right into the television cameras, asked more than 100 million Americans at the end of his famous debate against Jimmy Carter. Reagan won in a landslide.

This chapter documents how Trumponomics has outperformed Bidenomics on nearly every single economic/financial metric of side-be-side performance. The data is compelling, but there's another telling indicator: neither Joe Biden nor Kamala Harris nor any other Democrat running for office is still using the term "Bidenomics." Why is that? Because most Americans associate Bidenomics with failure. With higher prices for nearly everything. Economic stress. A lower standard of living. And a stack as high as the Washington Monument of Biden's unpaid bills. We titled our book in 2018 *Trumponomics*—because the policies were such a success that the term became synonymous with "prosperity." Bidenomics has become for many millions of Americans synonymous with "economic hardship."

The Trump economic miracle is easier to appreciate today than when he left office, because his successor has shipwrecked the economy. Just as the rule of politics is that just as you always want to follow a failure, your legacy is easier to appreciate if you are followed by a failure. By being slotted between Obama and Biden, it's easy for Trump to be seen as a success. And it helps that he was a success.

So let us start with the statistic that is the most problematic of all for Biden and Harris:

1) REAL TAKE HOME PAY UP UNDER TRUMP AND DOWN UNDER BIDEN

Throughout most of Biden's presidency inflation has outpaced wages and salaries for most families. So how can the White House claim that worker pay is rising?

The Biden PR flaks are playing a numbers deception: The White House is touting the rise of nominal hourly earnings, i.e., wages before inflation, since Biden took office. That part of the story is true. But as in the 1970s with double-digit inflation, nominal wages rose, but families got financially crushed because prices were rising so much faster. Today, prices have risen even faster, so those higher incomes buy less. Average weekly earnings after inflation are DOWN 4% under Biden while they were UP 10% under Trump.

The average worker in America is $2,100 POORER than when Biden came into office. This is the "affordability crisis" that is crushing families financially.

As the saying goes, this is game, set, match for the Trump economy over the Biden-Harris economy.

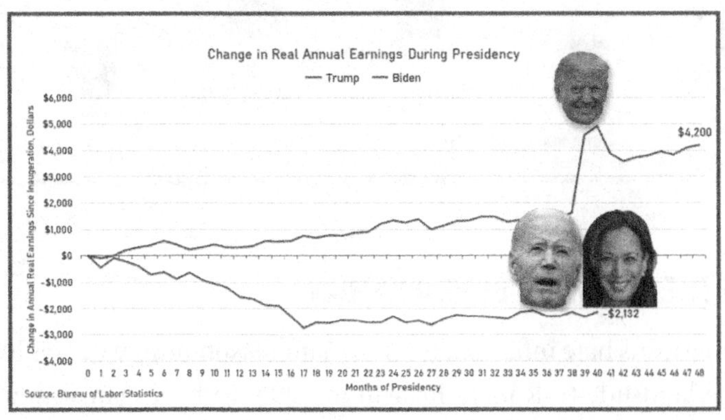

2) MEDIAN FAMILY INCOME MUCH HIGHER UNDER TRUMP

Another way to measure how families are doing is calculated every year by the U.S. Census Bureau—the gold standard of measuring how the economy is affecting the middle class. Under Trump—even accounting for Covid—the median family income rose by $5,800. That's the highest gain in real dollars than under any other president in history.

Under Biden, the data show that through 2022—the most recent data available, incomes FELL by more than $2,000. This is an astonishing $8,000 per household difference—in Trump's favor. The chart also shows that Trump's lift in middle income family earnings is higher than the other three most presidents record combined!

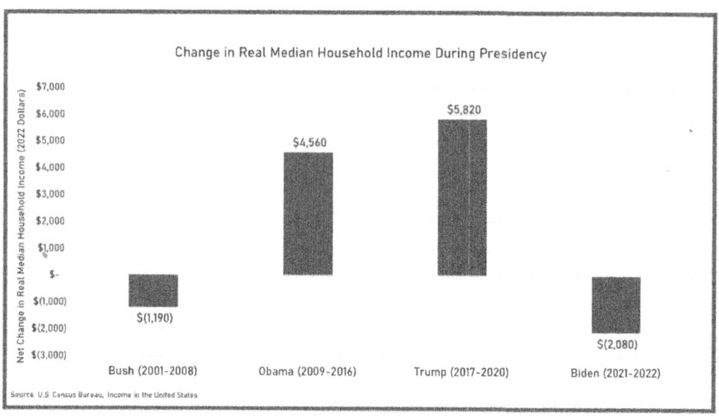

3) THE CURSE OF BIDENFLATION

Americans hate inflation. It is the main reason Jimmy Carter lost in a landslide to Ronald Reagan in 1980, with Reagan winning

42 states. That doesn't bode well for Harris, since she's been Vice President while the inflation rate has been higher than at any time since Carter was in office.

While Trump was president, the inflation rate averaged just a bit over 2% and the month he left office it had fallen to 1.5%—one of the lowest rates in 40 years. Biden has blatantly lied by saying that inflation was 9% when he came into office. Not even close.

Biden pushed through a $5 trillion spend and borrow and print money economic program. Within 18 months, the inflation rate had zoomed all the way up to 9.1%. How do you screw up the economy that quickly? Was he trying to ruin the American economy? Was he trying to emulate Jimmy Carter? Mercifully, the inflation rate has started to recede since the end of 2022, but the latest Bureau of Labor Statistics numbers indicate we are still seeing inflation rates of close to 3% to 4%, which is nearly double the Federal Reserve target rate of 2%.

Inflation 3x Higher Under Biden

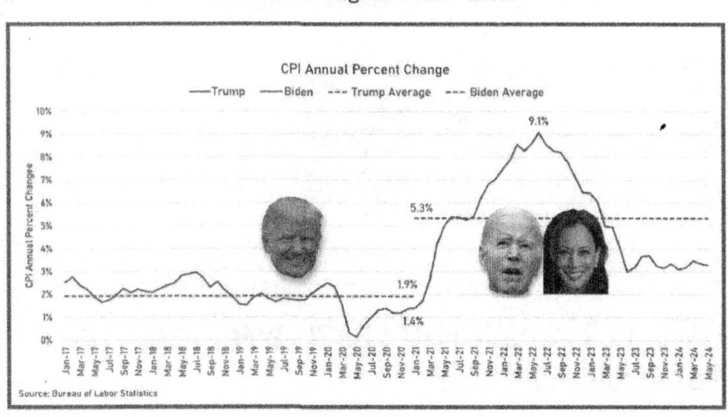

4) NECESSITIES OF LIFE FAR MORE EXPENSIVE UNDER BIDEN

Most people think that the inflation they face is a lot higher than the official 20% rise in prices. That is because the things that Americans HAVE to pay for every week—groceries, gas, rent or mortgage, insurance, tuition payments, health care and drug costs—have risen faster than the overall rate of inflation.

Even affordable fast food is now expensive. The CEO of McDonald's acknowledged that the price for a Big Mac Meal is now more than $10 and the average cost of a menu item is 40% higher than before the pandemic. The memorable $1 menu deals at McDonalds are now just that—a memory. Now McDonalds advertises a $5 value meal menu.

Essentials 3x to 5x More Expensive Under Biden

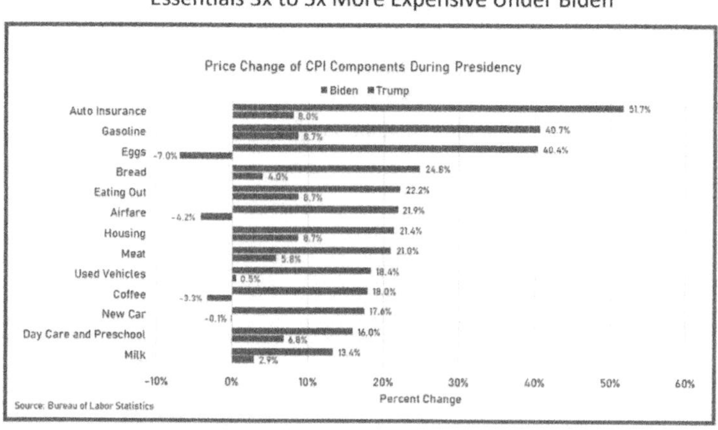

5) WORKER PRODUCTIVITY GAINS WERE EIGHT TIMES HIGHER UNDER TRUMP

Wages go up for workers when they can produce more on the job. This is the combination of a better educated and trained workforce and more capital—machinery, equipment, computers, robots—for workers to work with. Under Trump, worker productivity leaped forward. Under Biden we've seen record low productivity gains. CNBC reported at the end of 2022 that "worker productivity is falling at the fastest rate in four decades." We don't know why workers are less productive than they were under Trump. Some of the explanations include a slowdown in capital spending by businesses, stress, drug issues, burnout on the job, and possibly remote work.

Labor Productivity 10x Higher Under Trump

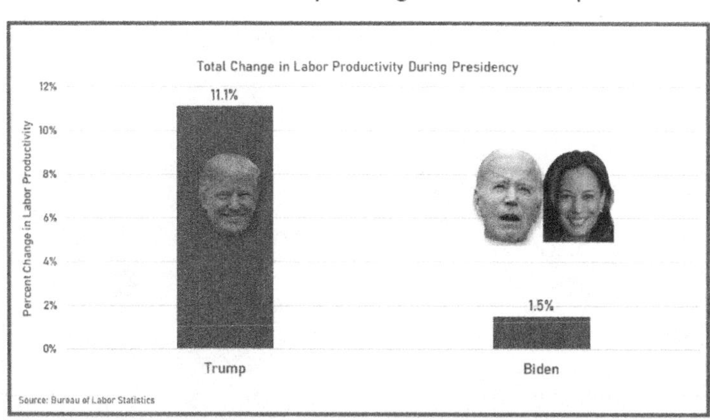

6) GAS PRICES SURGED UNDER BIDEN

Trump came into office promising a "drill baby drill" strategy. For the first time in more than 50 years, the U.S. was producing more oil and gas than it was consuming. Prices fell and America became an oil and gas exporter. Trump struck a symbolic blow as well by withdrawing the United States from the anti-American Paris Climate Treaty.

Biden came into office declaring war on American energy—and he's winning. He promised to kill off the American oil, gas and coal industry. His first act in office was to kill the vital Keystone XL pipeline so that American oil and gas could be transported to American communities. (This was the same president who said we needed to spend $1 trillion on infrastructure.) The gas price was $2.50 a gallon when Trump left office. Now in most markets it is $3.50 to $4.00 a gallon. In California, gas has been above $5 a gallon. Overall, energy prices rose 40% in the first 40 months of Biden's presidency.

Gas Prices A Dollar A Gallon Higher Under Biden

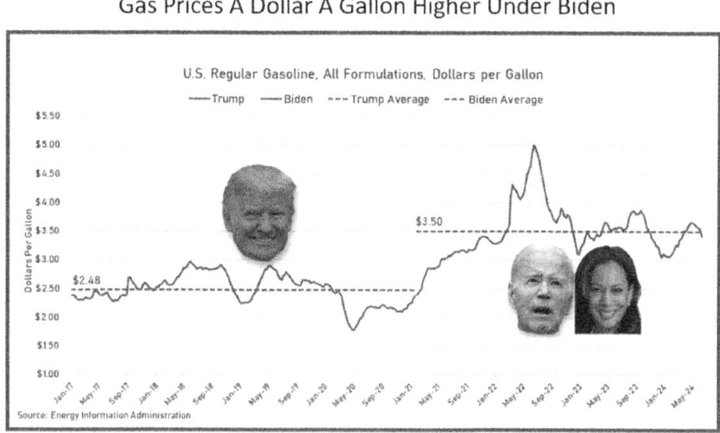

7) THE AMERICAN DREAM OF BUYING A HOME IS NOW UNAFFORDABLE

Home ownership in America has fallen under Biden after rising under Trump. One big reason is that average mortgage payments for a median value home have more than doubled in three and a half years under Biden. As such, the National Association of Realtors calculates that the affordability of housing has hit a 40-year low under Biden after affordability surged under Biden.

Monthly Mortgage Payments Have Doubled Under Biden

Biden has proposed a new government giveaway program to ease the problem that his own spendthrift policies caused. He will offer first-time home buyers an annual subsidy of $5,000 for two years. That's equivalent to a $416 per month taxpayer subsidy on mortgage payments. Many more of these programs and the government might as well be simply purchasing houses for families. Or perhaps Biden will propose mortgage loan forgiveness—as he's done for millions of young people who aren't paying back their student loans—and make the taxpayers pay off the debt.

But none of these solutions really address the root cause of the housing affordability crisis. What Biden fails to understand is that two factors impact homeownership rates: the interest rate and real income growth. Both of these are now working against first-time homebuyers.

8) MORTGAGE INTEREST RATES TWICE AS HIGH UNDER BIDEN THAN TRUMP

A major reason why buying a new home is so hard today is that the mortgage interest rate has spiked to 7% nationally, compared to 3% in 2020 when Trump left office. When the federal government is spending $7 trillion a year, this puts enormous pressure on inflation and interest rates.

Mortgage Rate 3% Under Trump, 7% Under Biden

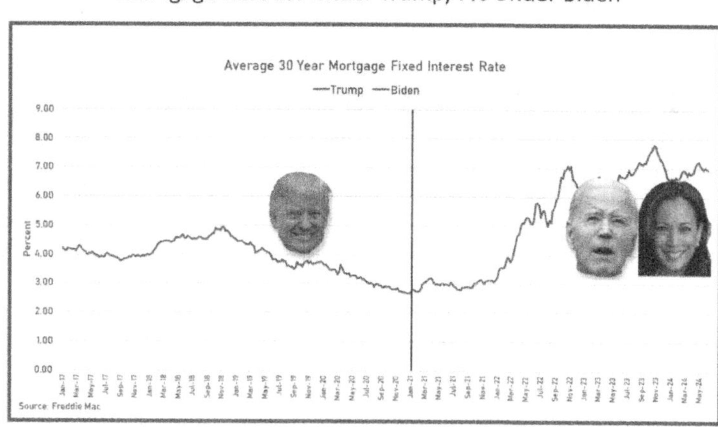

The American Dream of home ownership is yet another casualty of Bidenflation.

9) THE NATIONAL DEBT IS HEADED TO $50 TRILLION UNDER BIDEN

The national debt has risen rapidly under Republicans and Democrats. We hold both parties responsible for the sea of red ink in Washington. Trump was a big borrower. But no president perhaps ever has been as financially reckless as Joe Biden.

The government debt burden, which now stands at $34 trillion, is up roughly $6 trillion—already—since Biden came into office. This is roughly more money adjusted for inflation than we borrowed to fight and win World War II. If we take out the two Covid years of 2020 and 2021, when federal spending skyrocketed due to the catastrophe of shutting down businesses and schools, the average deficit was $750 billion a year under Trump and $1.5 trillion under Biden.

There has been some disagreement about who is more responsible for the rise of the national debt—Trump or Biden. To answer that question, we examined the Congressional Budget Office baseline for 2021-31 when Trump left office, versus what that same year 10-year forecast looks like as of June of 2024 since Biden came into office. What the data reveal is that the debt is $7 trillion HIGHER under Biden than it would have been if Trump had been reelected.

Biden Adds $7 Trillion To Debt

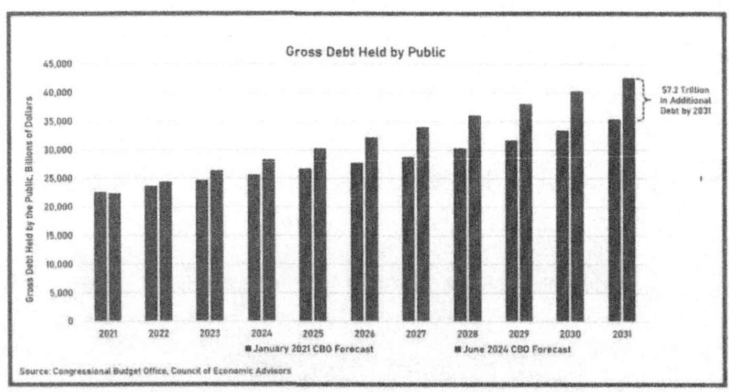

There has been no crisis or emergency under Biden—except for the crises he has created himself. Why are we borrowing such huge sums even though the COVID crisis ended three years ago? That debt burden is expected to rise to $50 trillion in 10 years even though the White House and Congress are pretending that they cut the debt. Over just the last 12 months, federal borrowing exceeded $2 trillion. This isn't progress.

Even Kamala admits that if she is elected, we will borrow close to $2 trillion a year for the next decade—consistent with the Biden baseline. It's scary: she doesn't even PRETEND to have a plan to get near a balanced budget.

10) TRUMP CUT TAXES, BIDEN AND KAMALA WANT TO RAISE THEM

As we have pointed out, the Trump tax cuts were one of the crown jewels of his agenda. We cut tax rates for businesses—from large corporations to small start-up firms on Main Street USA—to spur more economic activity and more jobs here at home for American workers. It's no accident that the unemployment rate fell so low that there was a shortage of workers in the wake of those tax rate cuts. Biden has promised to raise tax rates. His corporate tax plan would raise taxes higher than virtually any other country and far above the rate in China, Russia, and Europe.

The average family saved $2,000 a year on their taxes under the Trump tax plan. Those savings would go away if Biden keeps his promise to cancel the entire Trump tax plan.

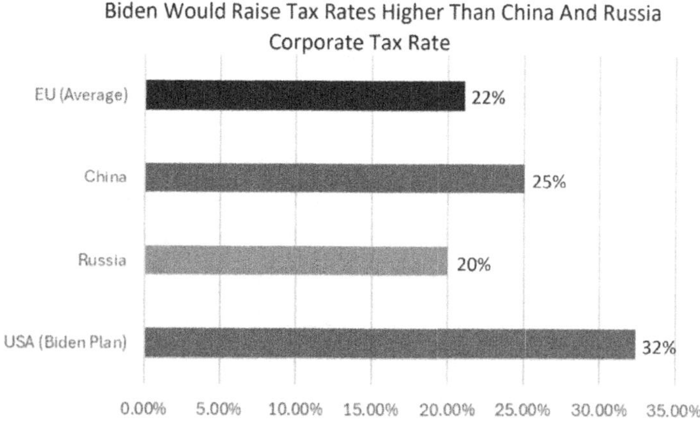

11) CREDIT CARD DEBT RISES TO ALL TIME HIGH UNDER BIDEN

Because prices of everything have soared under Biden, Americans are suffering from what we call "America's Affordability Crisis." The people who are hurt most are working-class families and retirees on a fixed income.

As a consequence, more Americans than ever are going into debt to pay their bills. In 2024, credit card bills surpassed $1 trillion for the first time ever. Delinquencies on credit card payments are starting to rise because parents don't have the money to pay the escalating bills. Credit card debt is now 50% higher under Biden than under Trump. The New York Federal Reserve Bank reported in May 2024 that credit card delinquency rates rose from 5% to 7% over just the past year.

Credit Card Debt Explodes Under Biden

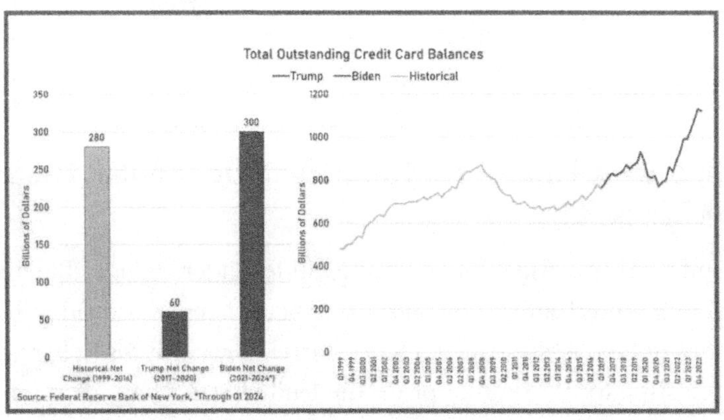

12) THE CRUSHING FINANCIAL BURDEN OF BIDEN REGULATIONS

In 2016 while running for president, Trump famously promised that he would "repeal two regulations for every new regulation enacted." He ended up killing more than four regulations of economic significance for every new regulation enacted. Next is the burden of Biden regulations. Under this administration, the modus operandi seems to be: if it moves, regulate it. Economist Casey Mulligan has found that Trump's deregulation initiatives saved the average family $45,000 (on a lifetime basis), Biden's regulatory spree has COST the average family $10,000. This is the hidden tax of the federal regulatory octopus.

Trump's Deregulation Saved Families $11,000; Biden's Re-Regulation Cost $47,000

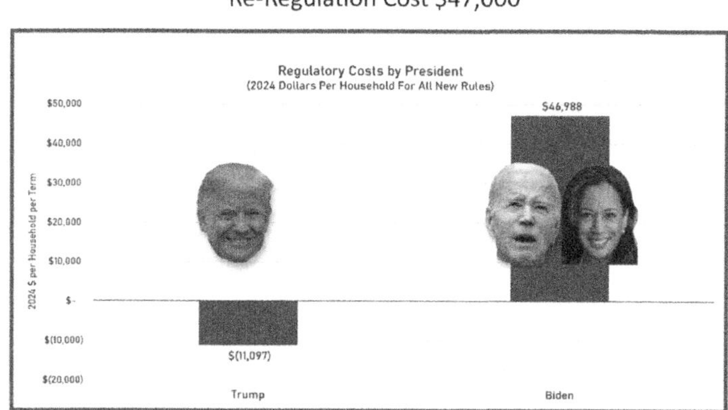

13) U.S. OIL PRODUCTION SURGED UNDER TRUMP, LAGS UNDER BIDEN

Under Trump, America was energy independent. Under Biden's war on American energy and his climate change obsession, the price of oil has surged from $50 a barrel to roughly $80 a barrel. Adjusting for this higher price, the United States has fallen well below the Trump baseline. We are losing about 3 million barrels a day, or almost $250 million a day in output.

Ironically, the Biden administration wants to bring anti-trust action against "big oil" executives for conspiring with OPEC to reduce supply and keep gas prices at the pump high.

But there is no one on the planet who has conspired to reduce oil and gas output more brazenly than Biden himself. If restricting oil and gas supply is a crime, maybe he had better put himself and Kamala behind bars.

This is the man who from the moment he came into office declared that he would bankrupt the oil and gas industry. The Biden Administration has enacted some 200 actions to limit oil and gas production here at home, as part of his climate change agenda and the "great transition" to zero fossil fuel production. Remember, one of Biden's first actions as president was to kill the Keystone XL oil pipeline.

A report from Unleash Prosperity finds that although oil production has risen in the last two years to about 13 million barrels daily, America could be and should be producing between two and three million more barrels per day if we had simply stuck with the Trump's pro-oil and gas strategy. The energy experts had predicted that we would be at 16 million barrels domestic production today.

Biden Slashes Oil Production By Three Millions of Barrels

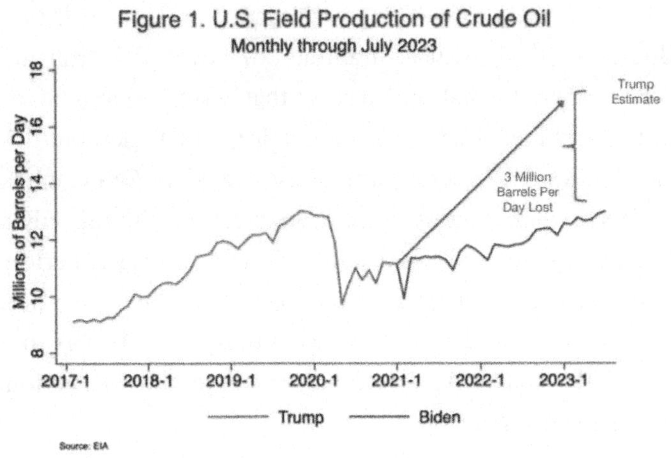

The Biden war on American oil and gas has cost American motorists and the overall American economy dearly. Over the past three and a half years our domestic production would have been almost 2.5 billion barrels HIGHER if Biden had simply left the industry alone.

What's doubly maddening is that Biden has played into the hands of the Iranians, the Russians and the Saudis, as if he was intentionally conspiring to make them money. Foreign dictators are enriched when we restrict our domestic supply because this raises the world price. By undermining shale activity in the U.S., we hand OPEC more monopoly pricing power, because we are no longer able to quickly respond to their production cuts with production increases of our own. Trump, by contrast, had brought OPEC to its knees.

Kamala opposes drilling as well. She's clearly got the support of Putin and Iran.

14) AMERICA'S ENERGY SECURITY IMPERILED BY BIDEN-HARRIS

To try to keep gas prices rising even faster than they already have, Biden—who is trying to impede efforts to drill for new domestic oil—is instead draining our Strategic Petroleum Reserve. This is the national reserve that is supposed to be tapped at times of a national crisis—a hurricane that takes out drilling capabilities or refineries, a terrorist attack, an OPEC embargo, and so on. But Biden is draining our reserves with the only crisis being his man-made decision to declare war on American oil and gas. Our reserves are now lower than they have been in more than a decade—and half what they were when Trump left office. This makes American vulnerable to potential serious oil and gas shortages.

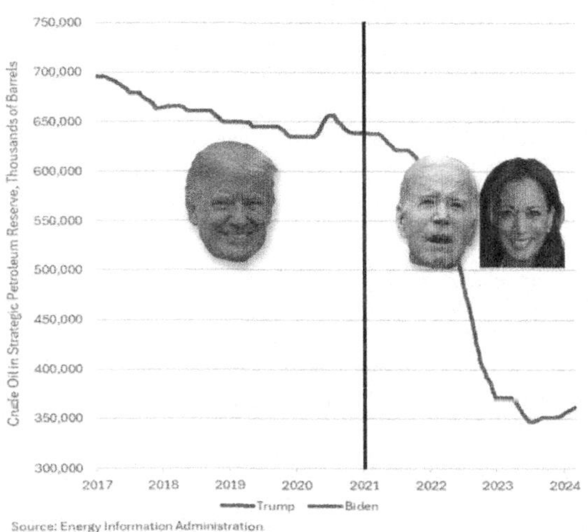

15) BIDEN'S WAR ON SMALL BUSINESSES

America's 33 million small businesses prospered under Trump. But since Biden has come into office, the NFIB "Small Business Optimism Index" could hardly be more depressing. It finds that the men and women who run small businesses and hire more than half of American workers are in a somber mood. The survey finds that small business confidence reached its lowest point in 12 years in April 2024.

Amazingly, small company CEOs are more fearful of the future today than even during the Covid pandemic when most businesses were shuttered. The index has fallen for most of the entire Biden presidency.

The confidence numbers have gotten worse every year Biden has been in office. Here are the numbers. Notice that as soon as Trump was elected the small business optimism index soared, and the minute Biden was elected small businesses went into a four-year funk.

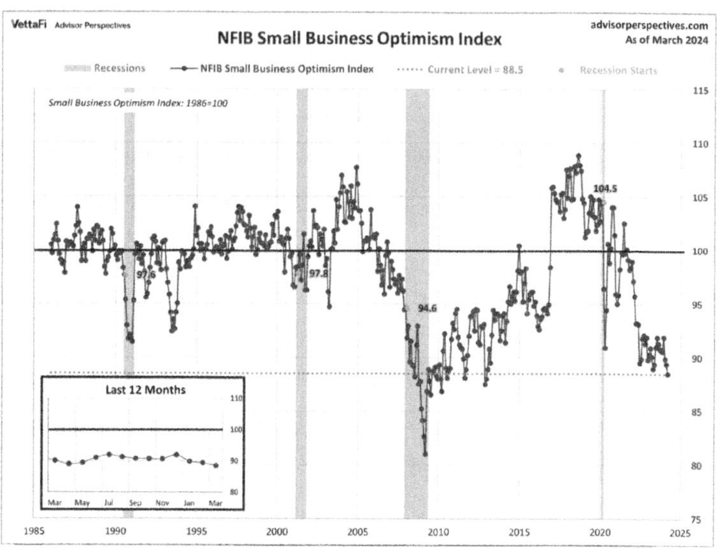

Here are the confidence numbers for the past four years:

March 2020 102.0
March 2021 98.2
March 2022 93.2
March 2023 90.1
March 2024 88.5

As an example of Biden's onerous rules and regulations aimed at small business, the Labor Department is threatening the franchise model whereby thousands of small entrepreneurs can start their own McDonald's or Arby's or retail store representing well known and trusted brands. They want the parent companies to be on alert that they can be sued for violations of labor laws, EPA edicts, or federal "diversity" requirements, or can be on the hook for lawsuits against their franchises.

This could be death of thousands of small and independent-owned franchises.

16) STOCK MARKET ROSE MUCH FASTER UNDER TRUMP THAN BIDEN

One myth constantly perpetuated by the media is that the stock market has performed better under Biden than Trump. That is only true in nominal terms. In after-inflation terms the stock market has done much better under Trump. By the way, people invest so that they can make money AFTER adjusting for inflation. Inflation erodes the value of stocks.

All three major indices have done better under Trump, as the charts below show. For example, after three years in office, the S&P 500 was up 35% after inflation under Trump, but only 9% under Biden.

S&P Returns Higher Under Trump

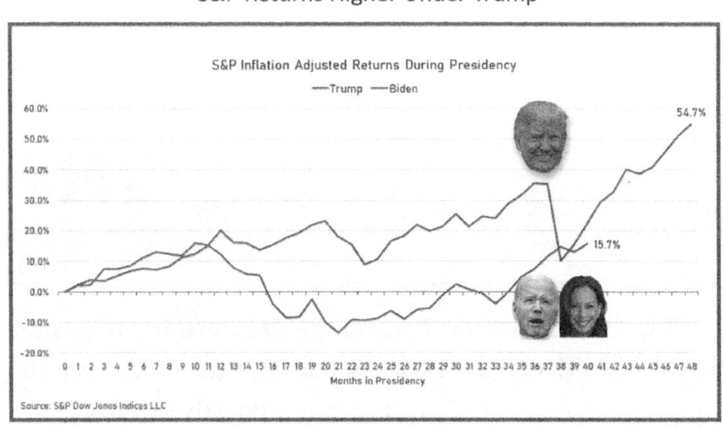

Nasdaq Returns Higher Under Trump

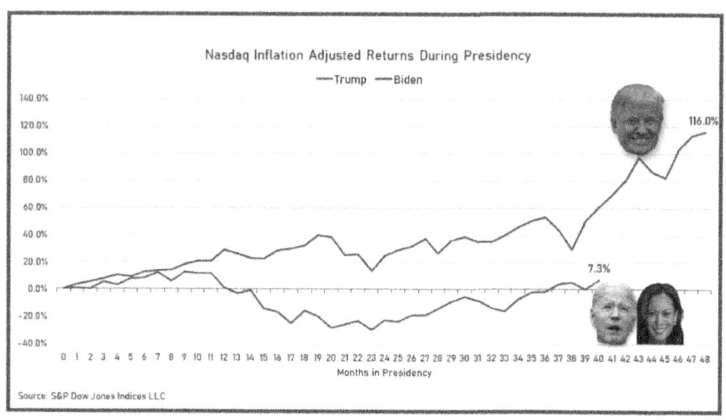

Dow Jones Returns Higher Under Trump

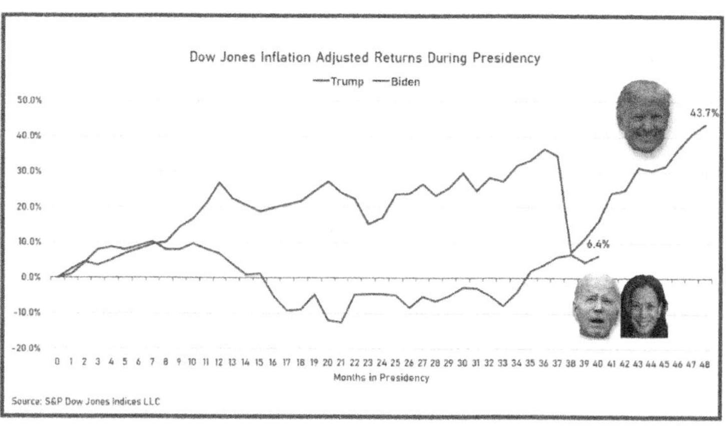

This matters not just because the stock market reflects the financial health of our businesses, but also because between 100 and 150 million Americans own stock, directly or through retirement accounts. The Nasdaq is up 8% under Biden and over the same time period was up 60% under Trump.

What this means is that 401k plans have done much better under Trump than Biden.

17) BORDER INSECURITY

Immigration is a positive force for the American economy, but it has to be through legal channels.

Trump ran for office promising to "build the wall" and stop illegal immigration. He succeeded in slowing the flow, but under Biden illegal immigration has been some four times higher than under Trump. Worse, the person in charge of the border was Kamala Harris. She presided over the greatest border disaster in American history. Scary to think of what happens if she is in charge of our nation's entire national security.

Legal immigration has been steady, but now illegal immigration exceeds legal entries. Biden reversed dozens of Trump's border security initiatives, such as "stay in Mexico" orders. Biden has not taken a single step to reduce illegal immigration, which is now estimated to be up by 7-10 million. The rate of deported illegal immigrants has been half as high under Biden as Trump even though the number of illegal crossings has soared.

Illegal Immigration Nearly Quadruples Under Biden

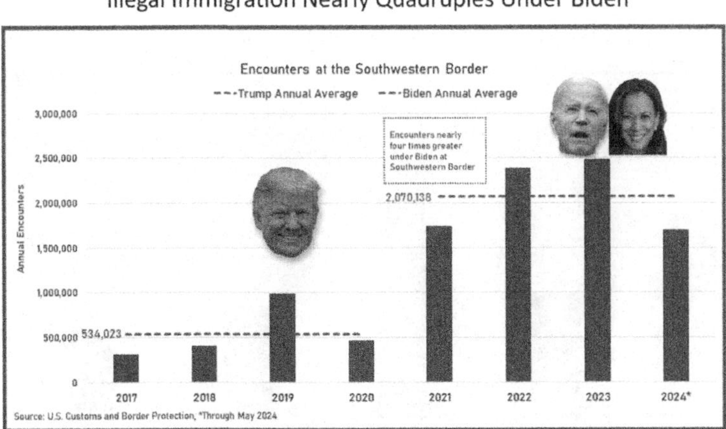

18) HOW AMERICANS RATE THE ECONOMY UNDER TRUMP VERSUS UNDER BIDEN

We don't have to ask statisticians or economists or political pundits if the economy is better or worse under Trump versus Biden. We can just ask the American people. Pollsters have been doing this for 50 years or more.

So how do Americans rate Trump's economy versus Biden's?

Polling is tricky because pollsters can jigger the questions to get the answers they want and sometimes you will get an outlier poll that skews in one direction or another. But there has been complete consistency in the polls on how Americans rate the economy. They almost all come to the same result for consumer confidence and outlook for the future economic conditions.

As the chart below shows, throughout almost the entire Trump presidency almost two of three Americans rated the economy as "good" or "great." Under Biden through May of 2024, almost two of three Americans rate the economy as "fair" or "poor."

The media may be trumpeting how well Biden is performing. But the public isn't buying it.

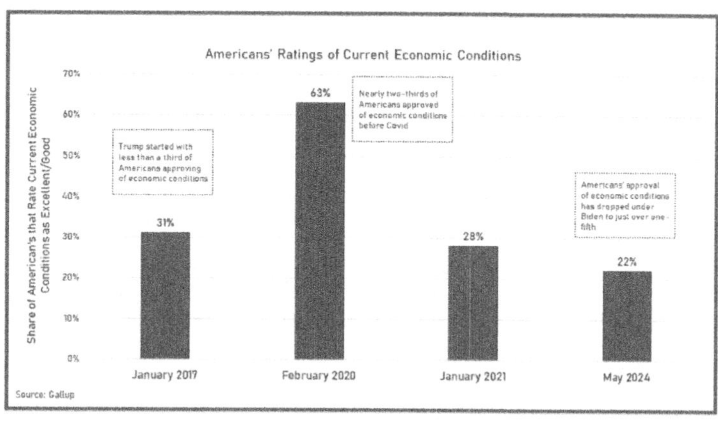

19) MINORITIES FARED MUCH BETTER UNDER BIDEN

The Left and the media keep charging ahead with this worn-out attack, but it's heavily refuted by the real world evidence of the past three presidencies.

The Census Bureau data show the biggest gains in income and the biggest declines in poverty for Hispanics and blacks happened under Donald J. Trump. Obama and Biden had much worse performances. Hispanic incomes rose slightly more under Obama than Trump, but that was only because Obama was in office for eight years and Trump has had only one term.

Amazingly, blacks gained more income under Trump than under Obama and Biden combined. In politics as in all things in life, you have to judge people on their results.

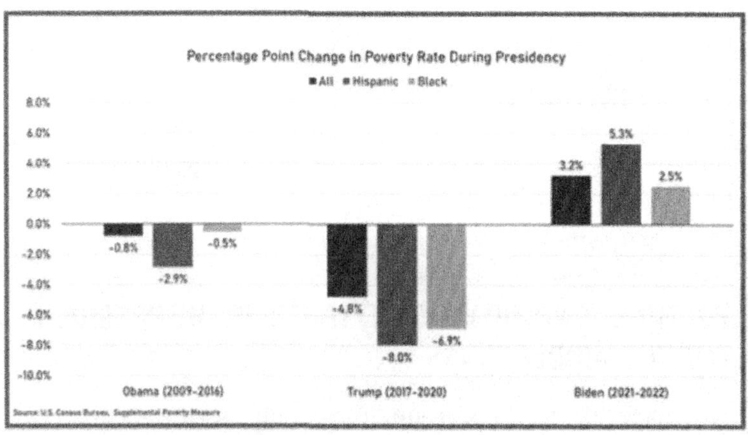

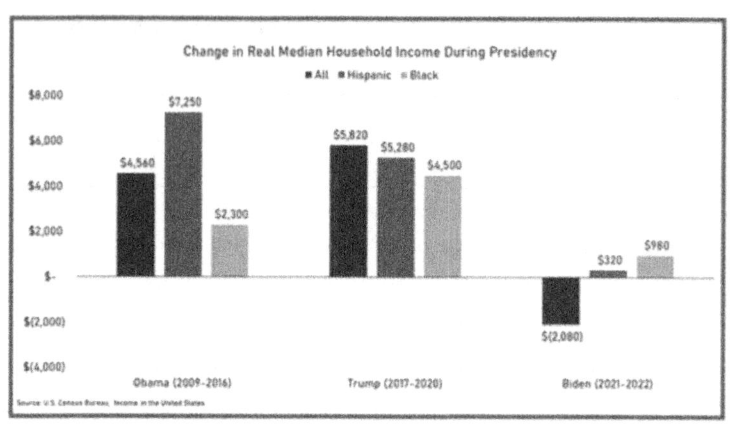

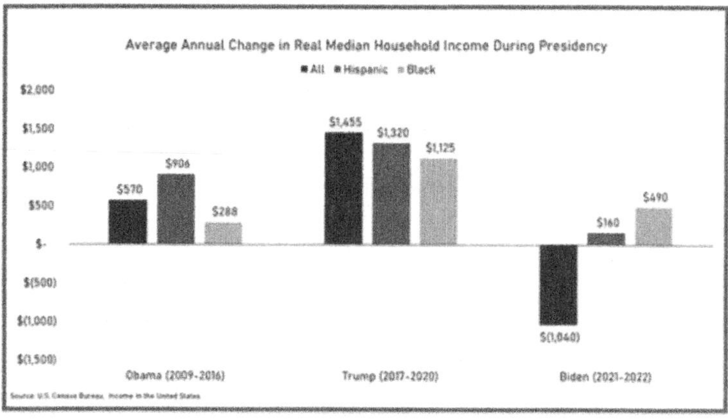

20) THE ECONOMIC VERDICT: TRUMP IS THE PRESIDENT FOR THE MIDDLE CLASS

Kamala is now running around the country saying she wants to "build out the middle class." That sounds like a familiar theme. It's exactly what Obama and Biden promised. But as the charts above show with compelling official government data, Trump beats Biden in delivering for working class Americans. This explains why virtually every poll from every pollster shows Trump with a 10 to 30 percentage point lead in the Question: Who is better to handle the economy?

All of the above indicators are harsh economic and pocketbook realities that Americans see and feel every day. They are almost all pointing in the direction of decline under Biden. One of the few areas where Biden has a strong record is on job creation. But even this is a bit of deception. Under Biden a much larger percentage of the jobs are part time, and one of the leading areas of employment growth has been in government/health care. Over the last eighteen months the U.S. had created more government/health care jobs than the total for manufacturing, construction, mining, warehousing, drilling, and transportation combined.

What's scary is that Democrats and Kamala don't seem to have any solution to these problems—or even an acknowledgement that they created them. Kamala blames "greedy corporations," or Putin, or Trump, or the Republicans in Congress, or even climate change.

Kamala Harris is a Malthusian pessimist—which is the worst possible type of person to provide leadership on American greatness and to give Americans confidence that we will have a more bountiful future. Not long ago, Kamala was asked why the economy is in trouble with home sales dropping to a 14-year low and mortgage applications at a 27-year-low. Here was her bumbling answer:

> "Young leaders" suffer from "climate anxiety." What is "climate anxiety?" It is "their fear about ... whether they should have children, whether they should ever think about buying a home for fear that it might

> be wiped out because of extreme weather occurrences."

How rich is this? So Kamala and the entire leftwing movement scare the bejesus out of our children with nonstop end-of-the-world indoctrination rhetoric on climate change. And then they wonder why millennials and Generation Xers are so paralyzed with fear that they won't invest in the future.

21) THE ECONOMY IS ONLY PART OF WHAT AILS AMERICA IN THE BIDEN-HARRIS REGIME

None of the economic measurements listed above include the litany of other not-so-easily-quantified indicators of hardship and national failing. They don't include the fact that peace under Trump has been replaced with two wars and maybe several others flaring up in the years to come—including China's potential takeover of Taiwan. They don't include the message of American weakness that Biden has signaled to the world with his tail-between-his-legs withdrawal from Afghanistan. It doesn't include that test scores in our schools have hit a 50-year low. Drug use and drug overdoses deaths have skyrocketed. Half of Americans have lost trust in our justice system in the wake of the Trump guilty verdict.

There is in America an overall sense of despair and despondence—a palpable gloom that has taken over the country. Fewer young Americans say they want to have kids, or believe in God, or believe in country. Many of our children truly believe that the end of days is coming because of climate change—an idea that has been planted in their heads since they were in kindergarten. The Biden-Harris administration has even said that "systemic racism is a stain on the nation's soul."

This doesn't feel like Ronald Reagan's Morning in America. Reagan had a famous saying: "strong at home, strong abroad."

Today, alas, we are neither.

CHAPTER 3

The Tax Cut Heard Round the World

"As with most things, President Reagan had it right. But Reagan was echoing the economic thoughts of President John F. Kennedy, who had already said, in 1962, and I quote, "The paradoxical truth is that the tax rates are too high today and tax revenues are too low, and the soundest way to raise revenues in the long run is to cut rates now…

"Reagan and Kennedy's views [on cutting taxes] prove that smart tax policy shouldn't be a partisan issue. It should be common sense. If you tax something you get less of it. It's as simple as that."

—Donald J. Trump, *Wall Street Journal*, May 1999

Whenever the two of us sat down with Donald Trump—from our very first meeting back in January of 2016—he was always fascinated with Ronald Reagan. Reagan was and still is the most popular and successful President of modern times, so it was natural that Trump was ever-curious about how Reagan adopted his policies and how he remains so beloved.

He still has that fascination and the Reagan envy. Let's face it. Reagan is a VERY good policy role model. The Reagan tax cuts and other Reaganomics policies unleashed a 25-year boom in America—creating a level of prosperity seldom matched in our history.

And though Regan and Trump are two stylistically very different people, they both shared a deep-rooted belief that the American people are boundless in their capacity to do good if unfettered by government. We believe firmly that it was the amazing success of the Reagan tax cuts that inspired Trump to reprise that agenda.

He had a good starting point, because just as Reagan followed the collapse of the economy under Jimmy Carter, Trump took over from eight years of economic doldrums under Obama. Obama had predicted 4% growth with his policies, and that never happened over two terms in office. People forget also that when Trump entered office, the economy was hobbling. The growth rates in 2016 were barely above 1%. Job creation was mediocre and the labor force participation rate remained woefully low. Companies were making profits, but they were sitting on capital and the reinvestment rate for businesses had flatlined.

Our line to Trump at that meeting (and to members of Congress whom we consulted with regularly) was that we needed an "anti-recession" insurance package of tax cuts. Trump agreed. (We may need one again in 2025!) We weren't the only ones saying this. Many economists on the left and the right were worried that the economy, feeble as it was throughout the Obama presidency, had run out of steam. Our view was policy mistakes under Obama on the tax, deficit and regulatory front had prevented a real recovery. The economy wasn't running out of gas, but rather had been bumping along for seven years without any policy pick-me-up with the exception of the sugar high of loose monetary policy of near-zero interest rates.

As newly tapped senior advisors in the early stages of 2016, along with the indispensable Larry Kudlow without whom the tax cut would not have happened, Trump tasked us to help design a tax plan that would maximize growth and jobs. It was a task we were honored to take on and we take great pride in the final product and the positive impact it has had on the economy in the five years since passage.

HOW TRUMP'S HISTORIC TAX PLAN HAPPENED

In our 2018 book, *Trumponomics*, the two of us chronicle in great detail how the tax bill was eventually passed into law. We won't repeat that story, but refer readers to that book, and here just highlight some critically important events.

This original Trump tax plan had been released at the end of September of 2015. There was no accompanying documentation to speak of. Trump was assuring voters his intention was to lower taxes and do so in a way that would help the economy grown.

The original plan proposed five tax changes:

1. Anyone who is single and earns less than $25,000 or is married and jointly earns less than $50,000 would not owe any federal income tax. This would remove more than one-third of households in the country from the income tax rolls.

   (Trump joked at a press conference in late 2015 that many tax filers would get a new one-page form to send to the IRS saying, "I win." This was posted on Trump's campaign website.)

2. Every American would see a "simpler" tax code with four brackets—0 percent, 10 percent, 20 percent and 25 percent—instead of seven.
3. Cut the corporate tax rate from 35 percent to 15 percent. No business in the U.S. would pay more than 15 percent of its business income in taxes—from a Fortune 500 to a mom-and-pop shop to a freelancer living job-to-job.
4. Bring back money that corporations are holding overseas to avoid taxation by imposing a one-time reduced 10 percent tax. That would return an estimated $2.1 trillion to the U.S. An immediate tax would be imposed on American companies' overseas earning—taxes that can currently be deferred.
5. Eliminate the marriage penalty, the alternative minimum tax and the estate tax—a 40 percent tax on inheritances of more than $5.4 million.

What is remarkable about that original outline of a tax plan is how close this was to the plan that he would sign into law a little over two years later. The eventual plan achieved dramatic and almost all positive tax changes. These included:

- Double the standard deduction from $12,500 to $25,000
- Cut the corporate tax rate from 35% to 21%
- Lower the repatriation tax on foreign earnings to 10%
- Eliminate the marriage penalty
- Eliminate the alternative minimum tax for most households
- Cap the state and local tax deduction at $10,000

- Reduce the small business tax rate from 39.6% to 24%
- Reduce the highest income tax rate from 39.6% to 37%
- Allow immediate expensing for many types of capital purchases and R&D
- Raise offsetting revenues by allowing drilling for oil in Alaska
- Repeal the Obamacare mandate requiring Americans to buy health insurance

It wasn't exactly the flat tax that the two of us have long advocated. But this was an astonishing and unlikely legislative triumph. More importantly, almost all the provisions made good economic sense.

THE TAX CUT'S CROWN JEWEL: A 21% CORPORATE TAX CUT

The chart you see below is one that helped change U.S. tax policy in a monumentally important way. Its impact will hopefully live on for years and decades to come.

It was the very first graphic that we showed Donald Trump at our first policy meeting with him in early 2016.

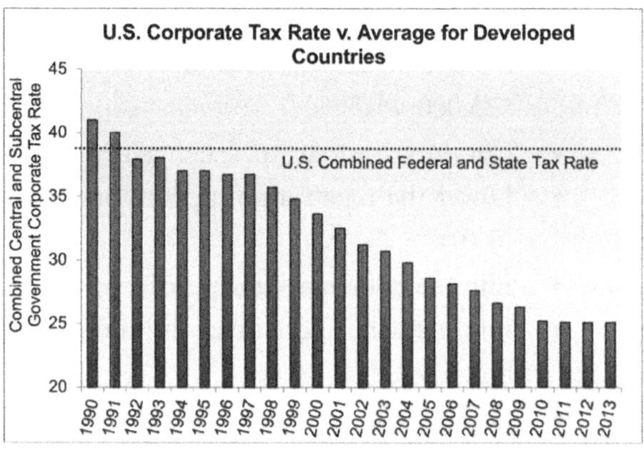

As soon as Trump saw this chart, he was astounded. We told him that this high corporate tax was much like "a tariff that we are imposing on our own companies." At that time, the U.S. tax rate of 35 percent (federal) and 40% total was the highest of all the nations we compete with. The rest of the world was at a rate closer to 20-25% with some nations like Ireland as low as 12.5%. He was 100% on board with getting the rate down as quickly as possible. He described our highest business tax rate as "a head start program" for other nations competing with the United States.

For years, everyone seemed to recognize this problem, but nothing got done to fix it—under Clinton, Bush or Obama. Even President Obama's own tax reform commission, headed by former Fed chairman Paul Volcker, found "deep flaws" in the corporate tax and concluded:

> "The high statutory corporate tax rate reduces the return to investments and therefore discourages saving and investment.... The tax acts to reduce the productivity of American businesses and American workers, increase the likelihood and cost of financial distress, and drain resources away from more valuable uses."

It would have been difficult to devise a corporate tax that did more to undermine America's national interest.

The corporate tax system was also completely unfair. Some industries, like retailers, paid close to 35%, while other companies, such as those in wind and solar energy, had a negative tax liability—i.e., they ate tax dollars, they didn't generate them. Many opponents of the tax cut argued that although the U.S. had a high statutory tax rate, the effective rate on average was very low. Actually, even our effective rate was higher than that of most nations. But the reason for the differential between the statutory and the actual rate paid was that many industries found ways to lower their rates to effectively zero. Our point was: let's get the rate down to 15% but make sure everyone is paying it.

Liberals like to pretend that the U.S. tax rates aren't chasing out businesses and jobs, but then why are all the nations we compete with slashing their rates? Why was tiny Ireland, with the lowest corporate tax rate, the fastest growing nation in Europe?

Over a 25-year period, the international average tax rate had come down from almost 40% in 1990 to closer to 20% by 2016. During this time, the U.S. rates hadn't budged, while the rest of the world kept chopping. We were like a 6th grader who stops growing and then goes out and tries to play competitive basketball with 22-year-olds over six feet tall.

We told Trump that the people who pay the biggest price for our economically masochistic tax system were the American workers. He immediately saw the logic in this. The corporate tax rate chased investment out of the United States—through a process called "inversions"—and thus lowered the wages of American workers. The chart below shows the historic 90% plus relationship between capital investment per worker and worker wages. More investment here in the U.S. means higher wages for Americans.

Even though we were sometimes dismissed as "supply side" zealots who had an out-of-the-mainstream view on the power of a corporate tax cut to help workers, the truth is we had more conventional economic analysts on our side. The World Bank had issued reports on the negative impact of high corporate rates. More importantly, the Congressional Budget Office, hardly a friend of tax cutting conservatives, had issued a report in 2016 that confirmed our view that workers would benefit. According to CBO, corporate tax "burdens are measured" using a set of economic assumptions that it described as "reasonable for the U.S. economy. Given those assumptions, domestic labor bears slightly more than 70 percent of the burden of the corporate income tax." In other words, cut the corporate tax burden and middle-class Americans will reap the rewards in higher pay checks and more jobs.

Our friend and colleague, Kevin Hassett, who would later lead President Trump's Council of Economic Advisers, and played a major role in providing the key research that made the case for the tax reductions, had also produced peer review studies showing that lower corporate taxes lead to higher real worker wages.

THE CONTINUING MYTH OF THE $6 TRILLION TAX CUT

Then as now, Democrats attacked the Trump tax plan as too expensive and too tilted to the rich. This is what Democrats had been saying about virtually GOP tax cut proposal since the Reagan years. The attack of fiscal irresponsibility often worked because many Republicans put a balanced budget and deficit reduction above all else. They also didn't truly understand the power of lowering tax rates on economic activity.

Neither did Hillary Clinton—or more recently President Biden, who back in 2016 routinely bashed the Trump tax plan as "trickle down economics." This class warfare card has become the standard and tired response to every Republican tax plan reform for 30 years. It was one reason we hadn't succeeded in cleaning out the stables of the tax code since the Reagan era. Democrats had no interest in cutting or reforming the tax system.

Not only did Hillary claim that the plan would "blow a $6 trillion hole in the debt," which was rich coming from someone who worked for an administration that nearly doubled the debt in eight years, but she even claimed that the cut would cost jobs and could even "cause a recession." Given that Democrats were mesmerized by the Keynesian idea that deficits are good, because they stimulate the economy by putting more money in people's pockets, this was an astonishingly hypocritical charge. All the more so because when Biden came into office, he spent $3 trillion, which was universally applauded by the same Democrats who had earlier complained that the Trump tax cuts were unaffordable.

CAPPING THE STATE AND LOCAL TAX DEDUCTION

One of the other gems of the tax plan was the capping of the state and local tax deduction. This was a tax deduction for millionaires in billionaires in high-tax blue states with tax rates of more than 10 percent. This list included California, New York, New Jersey, and Illinois. The deduction required lower- and middle-income tax filers in states like Florida, Tennessee, and Utah to pay higher taxes to subsidize the top one percent in income in the highest tax states. Also, by allowing millionaires to write off their state and local taxes, they were exporting up to 40% of the tax to residents of other states.

Democratic governors and some Republicans in blue states fought hard to save the full deductibility of what was called the SALT tax deduction. California's Gov. Jerry Brown called the provision "evil in the extreme" and he fumed that it would "divide the hell out of us." Now each state would have to pay the full freight for their high taxes.

We take personal pride in the fact that we were dogged on this issue and refused to allow blue state Republicans to bring back the deduction. There was intense pressure to fold, but we persuaded President Trump and the Senate Republicans this would only benefit rich people and make the income distribution tables look worse. We also pointed out that the Democrats were being hypocritical here: arguing to save a major tax loophole for the super-rich.

We argued that by eliminating the state and local tax deduction, we could broaden the tax base and lower the tax rates even more by nearly $1 trillion over the decade. We argued that among the biggest beneficiaries of this federal tax cut—which was about $2.5 trillion over 10 years—would be state and local governments. When the federal government doesn't take $2.5 trillion from the taxpayers of states, that's $2.5 trillion that stays in the local and state economies that never has to go to Washington in the first place.

After the tax cut was passed with the SALT limitation cap in place, we wrote an article for the Wall Street Journal that carried the following headline: "So Long, California. Sayonara, New York."

Our predictions could not have been more prescient and accurate:

> *Blue states will lose millions of people in the years to come—and they aren't ready.*
>
> As the Trump tax cut was being debated in December, California's Gov. Jerry Brown called the bill "evil in the extreme" and fumed that it would "divide the hell out of

us." He's right—but in the end, this change could be good for all the states.

In the years to come, millions of people, thousands of businesses, and tens of billions of dollars of net income will flee high-tax blue states for low-tax red states. This migration has been happening for years. But the Trump tax bill's cap on the deduction for state and local taxes, or SALT, will accelerate the pace. The losers will be most of the Northeast, along with California. The winners are likely to be states like Arizona, Nevada, Tennessee, Texas and Utah.

For years blue states have exported a third or more of their tax burden to residents of other states. In places like California, where the top income-tax rate exceeds 13%, that tax could be deducted on a federal return. Now that deduction for state and local taxes will be capped at $10,000 per family....

Now that the SALT subsidy is gone, how bad will it get for high-tax blue states? Very bad. We estimate, based on the historical relationship between tax rates and migration patterns, that both California and New York will lose on net about 800,000 residents over the next three years—roughly twice the number that left from 2014-16. Our calculations suggest that Connecticut, New Jersey and Minnesota combined will hemorrhage another roughly 500,000 people in the same period.

By the way, we also note that the winners in the national migration race for people would likely be states such as Arizona, Nevada, Tennessee, Texas, and Utah. Predictably, these states are among the prosperous today.

THE REAL RECORD OF THE TRUMP CUTS: AN ECONOMIC BOOM

That's a quick history of what was in the tax plan and how it was eventually signed into law by Donald Trump in late 2017. We wish to give a shout out to then-Senate Finance Committee chairman Orin Hatch of Utah. He played a vital role in getting this bill signed into law. Senator Hatch died two years ago without seeing all the positive results of his handiwork.

More than six years have gone by so let's fast forward to today and examine how the tax plan worked. For five years the Democrats have berated the plan as a giant tax cut for the rich with no economic benefits. What does the actual evidence show?

Right out of the gate, the Trump tax cut awakened the American economy to its potential as if he had twisted the ignition switch on a Ferrari.

Trump's policies, in just the first year, restructured the American economy. As our colleague Larry Kudlow put it, "We've moved from secular stagnation (i.e., high taxes, massive regulation, huge government spending, and a disdain for business and investors) to a new private-sector incentive system that *rewards* success."

The keys to success were slashing individual and corporate tax rates, providing 100% immediate expensing for plants and technology, and making it easy for big companies who fled our high-tax system to bring the money back home. The war against business and investment ended overnight.

When we would see President Trump after the tax bill passed, and he asked us whether it was working, we would respond, "even better than we expected." And he would reply, "Not better than I expected." He was a true believer.

In just the first the 18 months after the tax bill became law, more than 250 American companies announced gigantic investment projects (Apple's projects were valued at $350 billion), paid sizeable bonuses to their workforces, increased 401(k) contributions, and raised corporate minimum wages and other benefits.

The stock market rally was shot out of a cannon with $7 trillion in new wealth. All the critics could say was that the gains went to shareholders through stock buybacks. They don't seem to understand that some 150 million Americans directly or through worker pension plans own stock.

Democrats then claimed that only crumbs were left for workers. But after the tax cut, Walmart—which has bitterly fought attempts to raise the federal minimum wage—raised its internal minimum wage for virtually all its wage employees, gave bonuses of up to $1,000, expanded maternity and parental leave, and committed $5,000 to every employee who adopts a child.

THE RICH PAID MORE

The latest IRS data on who bears the income-tax burden demonstrates yet again the benefits of lower tax rates over higher rates. Bernie Sanders should pay attention.

When President Donald Trump entered office, the richest 1% of tax filers ($675,000 of income and above) paid a little more than 40% of the income taxes collected. The 2017 Trump tax cut reduced the effective highest federal tax rate to 37% from 42%. The most recent (2024) IRS tax return data (for 2021) confirm that even as these rates were lowered—not to mention the corporate tax rate cut from 35% to 21%—the share of the tax burden shouldered by the top 1% ratcheted up to almost 46%—the highest share in modern times, and perhaps ever.

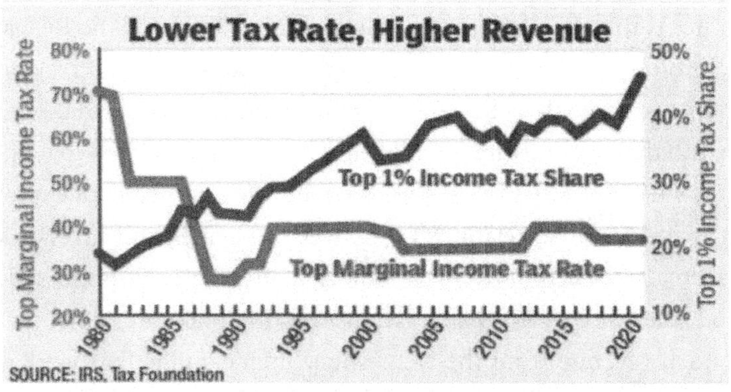

Data prove it: The Trump tax cuts soaked the rich

By Arthur Laffer and Stephen Moore
Published Feb. 29, 2024, 6:38 p.m. ET

Why was everyone caught by surprise by this? High-income earners shelter less and earn more when top tax rates fall. That shouldn't astonish anyone.

The chart below shows the inverse relationship between the highest tax rate applied and the share of taxes paid by the rich. When Ronald Reagan was elected president, for example, the top income tax rate in the United States stood at 70%. The wealthiest 1% of tax filers paid roughly 19% of the income tax. When Reagan cut that rate to 50% and then all the way down to 28% in 1987 (a tax reform nearly every senator—including Al

Gore, Ted Kennedy and Joe Biden—voted for) the share of taxes paid by the rich rose to 25%.

Think about that: When the highest tax rate was 70%, the rich paid less than 20% of the tax burden. With today's tax rate of 37%—or about half the rate during the 1970s—the top 1% pay almost half of all income taxes. And our data show that when the top tax rate stood at 91% in the early 1960s, before the Kennedy tax cuts, the top 1% paid only 15% of the taxes. This is all chronicled in "Taxes Have Consequences: An Income Tax History of the United States, by Laffer, Brian Domitrovic, and Jeanne Sinquefield." Another great history of the impact of income tax rates is the book by Larry Kudlow entitled "JFK and the Reagan Revolution." Kudlow reminds us of a famous line from President Kennedy shortly before he was assassinated: "It is a paradoxical truth that tax rates are too high and tax revenues are too low, and the soundest way to raise the revenues is to cut the tax rate now."

This inverse relationship between tax rates and taxes paid seems counterintuitive and almost mathematically impossible, but there are several explanations why high tax rates don't raise much revenue from the rich. The primary one is that workers work and investors invest more when the after-tax return is higher. Second, when tax rates are high, deductions to avoid paying those high rates become far more attractive to high-income earners, and they creep into the system as sure as crumbs on the kitchen floor attract mice. Third, people move to avoid paying high tax rates, and we've seen that in spades with the migration out of New York and California with the highest tax rates to Florida and Texas with no income tax.

We find it highly ironic that the same Democrats who want to raise the federal tax rate to 50% or 60% and even 70% to force the rich to "pay their fair share" are also the loudest voices in Congress for bringing back the biggest tax favor for the super-rich ever devised: the deductibility of state and local taxes. Green-energy tax write-offs provide massive shelters for the rich too.

High tax rates also send economic activity and taxable income offshore to lower-tax nations. This is how Ireland has become one of Europe's highest-performing economies.

And finally, high tax rates act as a financial penalty on economic activity and investment, which slows growth. When that happens, there are fewer rich people with smaller income gains to siphon off.

TRUMP TAX CUT KEPT AMERICAN COMPANIES HERE AT HOME

One of our goals when we designed the original Trump tax cut in early 2017 was to stop American companies from fleeing the U.S. and moving headquarters and factories and jobs overseas. Under Obama dozens of major companies engaged in tax inversions, which happen when companies move their headquarters to take advantage of lower tax rates outside the U.S.

America had the highest corporate tax rate in the world at 40% while the rest of the world was at closer to 20% and some countries were at or below 15%.

By cutting the federal corporate tax rate from 35% to 21%, the incentive to pack up and leave the United States was greatly diminished.

The policy was an astonishing success. The chart below shows that the number of inversions went to zero after the Trump tax cut. According to former House Ways and Means Committee chairman Kevin Brady, there was not a single inversion from 2018-22.

The companies stayed here and the jobs stayed here, unless Kamala is elected and pushes for the rate to return to 28%—or higher.

Corporate Inversions Before and After Trump Tax Cut

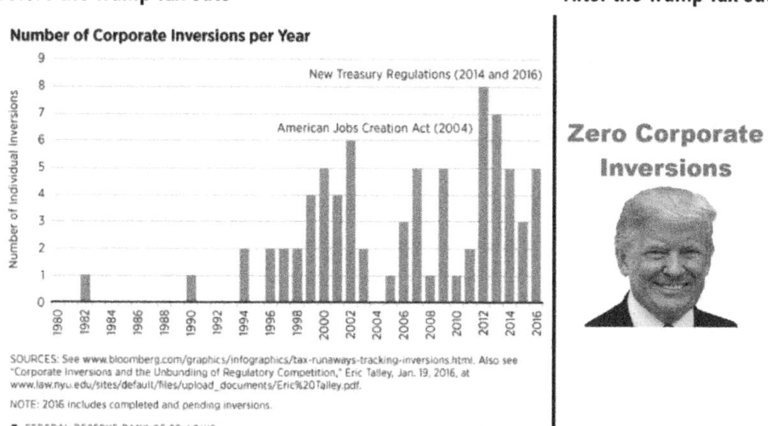

TRUMP TAX CUT ENDED THE DREADED ALTERNATIVE MINIMUM TAX

Trump all but eliminated one of the most obnoxious taxes ever invented—the so-called alternative minimum tax. Prior to the Trump tax cut, about five million Americans were ensnared by this tax. Many millions more had to fill out the AMT forms to see if they were subject to the penalty. But under Trump, the number of AMT filers fell to 200,000, according to the Urban Institute-Brookings Tax Policy Center. Most of this relief went to American families making $80,000 to $300,000.

This virtual elimination of the dreaded and unfair AMT was one of the unsung achievements of the Trump tax cut. The AMT was invented back in 1969 and targeted a small number of super-rich Americans who had found clever ways to avoid paying any income tax. But instead of ensnaring just millionaires and billionaires, it mostly hit people who were not rich.

The Democrats want to repeal the Trump tax cut and bring back the AMT. Under their plan, more than seven million Americans will pay the tax starting in 2026.

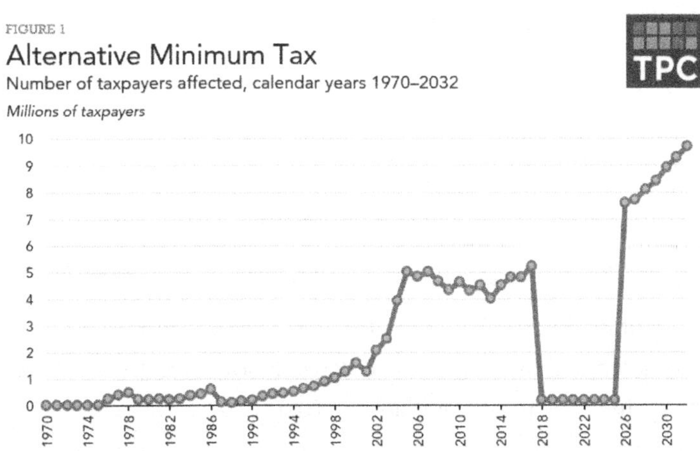

THE TRUMP TAX CUT INCENTIVIZES STATES TO CUT THEIR TAXES

Just as Laffer and Moore had predicted, the impact on high tax states has been highly negative and the impact on the low tax states has been highly positive.

This chart below shows the winners and losers:

Ten states with the most and least net domestic population migration from July 2021–July 2022

Bottom 10		Top 10	
California	-343,230	Florida	318,855
New York	-299,557	Texas	230,961
Illinois	-141,656	North Carolina	99,796
New Jersey	-64,231	South Carolina	84,030
Massachusetts	-57,292	Tennessee	81,646
Louisiana	-46,672	Georgia	81,406
Maryland	-45,101	Arizona	70,984
Pennsylvania	-39,957	Idaho	28,639
Virginia	-23,952	Alabama	28,609
Minnesota	-19,400	Oklahoma	26,791

Notice that the five states that have lost the most population have been the five highest tax states. Notice that the five states that gained the most population have the lowest income taxes—with three of the five—Texas, Tennessee, and Florida—having no income tax at all. These population/migration trends have continued in 2022 and 2023.

To understand why the outmigration from high tax states has accelerated, the loss of the federal tax deduction on states like California, New York and New Jersey has meant that wealthy tax filers in these states are now paying a higher effective tax rate. In California and New York, the highest income tax rate has increased to 13% from closer to 8%. In New Jersey the effective tax rate has risen to 10% from 7%.

We would have thought that the blue states would have responded by lowering their tax rates. Instead, states like Massachusetts and New Jersey have RAISED tax rates, which is akin to sailing right into a tsunami. Blue states are paying a high price for pretending that tax rates don't matter.

THE MYTH THAT MAKING THE TRUMP'S TAX CUTS PERMANENT WILL CAUSE INFLATION

The Democrats and the media have joined forces by attacking Trump's tax cuts as "inflationary." That's a bit of a weird line of argument because in the two years after the tax cuts were passed, prices fell to close to their lowest levels in modern times, and it wasn't until Biden came into office that inflation exploded.

But that hasn't stopped the rhetorical spray of sniper assaults from the Biden White House and the Kamala Harris campaign. The Biden White House complained in May of 2024 that the Republican push to extend and deepen the Trump tax cuts represents "a MAGAnomics economic agenda that would trigger an 'inflation bomb.'" The *New York Times* soon thereafter echoed that charge citing Wall Street and academic economists opposed to Trump.

The Biden team also has charged that Trump supports the tax cuts because he is trying to "protect the same corporations who are ripping off the American people with high prices, refusing to lower costs even as they make record corporate profits."

We're not sure why corporate profits are a bad thing—they sure beat corporate losses. Most Americans own U.S. corporations so more profits mean more money in our 401k plans for retirement years.

But recent history proves these charges are completely upside down.

Tax cuts reduce inflation, they don't increase it, as not only the Trump, but also the Reagan tax cuts have proven. Look what happened to inflation after the Reagan tax cuts in 1981.

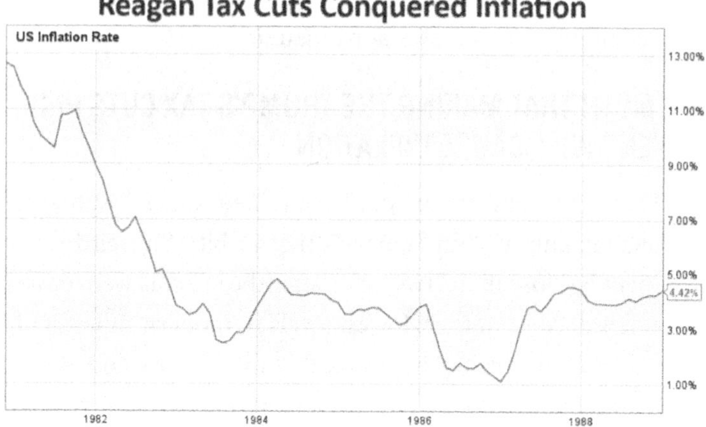

As Larry Kudlow has noted: "When marginal tax rates were slashed under JFK, Reagan, and Trump, inflation never uttered a serious peep."

After all these years, liberal Democrats still don't understand the supply side of the economy. The Reagan tax cuts caused a surge of investment and output. As the economy produced more of everything—from potato chips to microchips—prices fell. Prices rise when there is scarcity of goods, not a surge in production.

Which brings us to the Trump tax cuts. The argument goes that if Trump makes the tax cuts permanent, this will cause the deficit to rise and then prices will rise. Except that revenues did not fall after the Trump tax cuts. They rose. Corporate tax rates fell from 35% to 21% but the corporate tax collections have risen by more than 50% since 2017. This is because companies brought many of their money and operations home when the tax rate was lowered.

As we showed in the previous chapter, inflation under Trump was very low in all four years in office. The big surge in inflation happened AFTER Trump left office and Biden launched his multi-trillion spending spree.

TRUMP CORPORATE TAX CUTS DID NOT CAUSE THE $2 TRILLION BIDEN DEFICITS

Democrats say the number one reason for the stratospheric budget deficits under Biden is the Trump tax cut of 2017.

A major feature of that tax law was to lower the U.S. corporate tax rate from 35% (the highest in the world) down to slightly below the world average of 21%. This and other incentive features of the bill brought approximately $500 billion back to the United States. This money was taxed here not in foreign and offshore hideaway accounts.

Here is the most recent analysis of the corporate tax collections in billions of dollars:

Federal Corporate Tax Receipts

In Billions of Nominal Dollars
2017: 297
2018: 205
2019: 230
2020: 212
2021: 372
2022: 425
2023: 420
2024: 569 (estimate)

Yes, in the first two years of the tax cut, there were revenue losses as businesses and the U.S. economy writ large adjusted to the lower taxes.

But two years later, the economy adjusted and revenues climbed. Does that look remotely like a revenue LOSS to you?

The chart below is based on the latest comprehensive federal tax data. It is a handy refutation to the "tax cuts for the rich" mantra of Team Biden. Overall, after the Trump tax cuts were enacted in 2017, income tax collections rose. The share of income taxes paid by the rich soared, and the share of taxes paid by the bottom 50% fell.

In other words, the Trump tax cuts made the tax system more progressive, and the left still isn't happy. When reality conflicts with theory, liberals go with the theory.

Income Tax Shares Before and After TCJA

	Total Personal Income Taxes Paid (billions)	% of Total Paid By Top 1% of Income	% of Total Paid By Top 10% of Income	% of Total Paid By Bottom 50% of Income
2016	$1,442	37.3%	69.5%	3.0%
2021	$2,193	45.8%	75.8%	2.3%

https://www.irs.gov/pub/irs-soi/21in41ts.xls

SUMMARY: SIX REASONS TO MAKE THE TRUMP TAX CUT PERMANENT

At the heart of Trump's second term agenda will be to make his 2017 tax cut bill permanent.

He has a solid economic case on his side for doing so. Below we assimilate the latest official government data on how the tax cuts impacted jobs, the economy, tax fairness, and the simplicity of the tax code.

1) The Trump tax law was one of the biggest middle class tax cuts in U.S. history. The Trump Treasury Department calculated that it saved the average family of four

roughly $2,000 a year. This means, sorry Joe, repealing the bill would raise taxes for most families making less than $400,000. The House Budget Committee has estimated that the typical family will pay $1,500 more taxes annually if Biden repeals the Trump tax cut.

2) The Trump tax cuts vastly simplified the tax code for the majority of Americans. A major feature of the bill was to double the standard deduction from $12,500 to $25,000. As a result, prior to the Trump tax cuts, about one-third of tax filers had to itemize their deductions and keep track for the IRS of shoe boxes of receipts and other transactions related to mortgage payments, charitable deductions, interest payments, and so on. Now nearly 90% of Americans—and almost all middle- and lower-income families—just check a box of the standard deduction.

3) The Trump tax bill forces millionaires and billionaires in blue states to pay their fair share of taxes. One of the smartest features of the Trump bill was to cap the deduction of state and local taxes for the super-rich. This allowed millionaires and billionaires in blue states like New York and California to pay billions of dollars less taxes than an equally wealthy tax filer in low tax states like Florida and Texas. The old law encouraged states and localities to raise their taxes because it shifted the federal tax burden on to residents of other states.

4) The Trump tax cut expanded the economy and business activity, which meant HIGHER tax revenues. A study by Heritage Foundation fiscal analyst Preston Brashers examined the impact of the Trump tax cuts after four years and found that the policy changes ac-

tually raised MORE revenue in its first four years than the Congressional Budget Office predicted without the tax cut. The House Budget Committee similarly concluded in a May 2024 analysis that, "The Trump tax cuts resulted in economic growth that was a full percentage point above CBO's forecast." Revenues were $200 billion a year MORE than was predicted before the tax cuts.

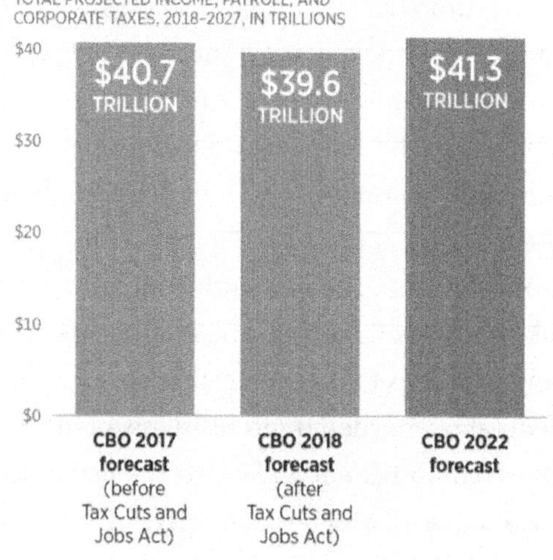

5) Kamala Harris is charging that the Trump tax cuts "benefited the rich" and are "unfair to the middle class." Except that the rich paid more taxes, not less, after the Trump tax cut. Joe Biden says continually that the major reason the deficit has exploded is that Trump cut taxes on the rich. Wrong. Five years after the Trump tax cuts, the IRS's own data show the top one percent of earners in America saw their percentage of total income taxes collected rise from 40% to 46% of the total in 2022. This was the LARGEST share of taxes paid by the rich EVER.

You've probably heard the lie by left-wing academics and activists that the wealthy pay a lower tax rate than the middle class. This is the argument by Warren Buffett that he pays a lower federal tax rate than the middle class. It's not true. The U.S. tax system even AFTER the Trump tax plan became law remains highly progressive. The higher the income, the higher the percentage of income that is paid in federal income tax as shown in the chart below.

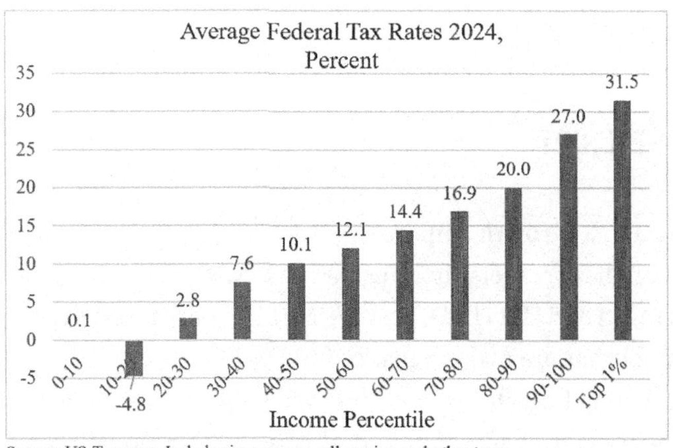

Source: US Treasury. Includes income, payroll, excise, and other taxes.

6) Small businesses benefited from the Trump tax cuts. Small businesses are the spinal cord of the U.S. economy. Most small businesses saw a 20% reduction in their tax rates under the Trump tax cut. Biden's plan to reverse those tax cuts would be the largest tax INCREASE on America's 30 million small businesses in the history of our country. There are no jobs without small businesses.

Now dear readers, you are equipped with the facts. This debate about the Trump tax cuts will go on for at least many more months and perhaps many years given the hot division between the two parties on this issue. We suspect that much of the opposition from Democrats is simply a result of the fact that this was a Trump policy—and so it must be wrong. What we have tried to lay out in these pages is why the objections are almost all wrong. Kamala Harris has come out guns blazing against the tax cut extension. She says going back to the old tax system that benefited the swamp, tax accountants, and our foreign rivals more than anyone else is her top priority. We doubt she will pay attention to the facts as her ideology stands in the way. But voter should if we want a return to American prosperity.

POSTSCRIPT

The 3.5% Growth Imperative

We can hear readers shouting: WHAT ABOUT THE DEFICIT? WHAT ABOUT THE DEBT? We NEED higher taxes! Even some Republicans are making that claim.

Trump has often told us, and said publicly, that his goal is 4% growth. As we have often said: this is an aspirational president.

The media scoffs at his big ideas like 4% or even 3% growth. But why are they so disdainful of a perfectly achievable goal.

Imagine if John F. Kennedy's advisors had told him in 1961, we will never put a man on the moon. Or what if Ronald Reagan's advisors had assured the Gipper that the Cold War was unwinnable and the United States should sue for peace. Actually, many naysayers told JFK and Reagan exactly these things, but fortunately these presidents followed their visionary instincts.

Donald Trump seems to be greeted by nattering nabobs of negativism in the media and academia every time he announces a policy goal. They say to him, "You can't build a wall. You can't keep out illegal immigrants. You can't root out the waste in government. You can't get Europe to pay more for its own defense. You can't make America energy independent." And on and on.

The one thing Washington is very good at is giving every excuse under the sun for why achievable things can't get done. The media and the Democrats say 4% growth is impossible. We would note that there is a very bizarre "degrowth" wing of the modern "progressive" movement that believes growth is the genesis of the problem in America. They think there is too much production, too much income, too many things, and too much wealth in America. Many of our environmental and inequality concerns would go away if everyone just got a little poorer.

Today, these are outliers in the Democratic party. But if you have a significant minority inside your clubhouse who don't even want the economy to expand, don't be surprised if it doesn't.

So back to the question of whether Trump's goal of 4% growth is achievable. Here history can be a guide. In the 1960s, after the Kennedy tax cuts were implemented, the economy grew by 4 percent annually from1965 to 1969), while unemployment sank to record lows, and a gold-linked dollar held down inflation.

In the 1980s, following the Reagan tax cut, the economy expanded at annual clip of closer to 3.75 percent (from 1983-89). Back then, economist Paul Samuelson, a Nobel laureate, declared that if the Reagan agenda were to produce high growth in outcome and jobs with declining inflation it would be "a miracle." The miracle happened. As we move deeper into the 21st century and the miracles of robotics and artificial intelligence, we have the potential of breaking into a new normal of faster growth.

Why does growth matter so much?

Growth is good because it leads to more prosperity for all citizens. But economic growth is also the key to expanding the treasure chest of trillions of dollars of additional private sector assets and government tax collections.

Yes. We CAN grow our way out of our problems. We can bend the debt curve down once we achieve 3% growth (we've averaged half that level under Biden) and we can put debt on a rapid descent with 3.5% growth. This means that anything that boosts growth—tax cuts, repealing inefficient regulations, pro-growth immigration policies, technology enhancers, privatization, pro-American energy policies, artificial intelligence, fixing our education system with school choice—has to be the highest public policy priority. A rising tide really does lift all boats. Trump believes that and so do we.

Growth will make future generations of Americans much richer, will erase deficits, and eventually the debt will shrink, as shown in the chart below from our economic advisory board member, Louis Woodhill. This is the essence of Trumponomics 2.0.

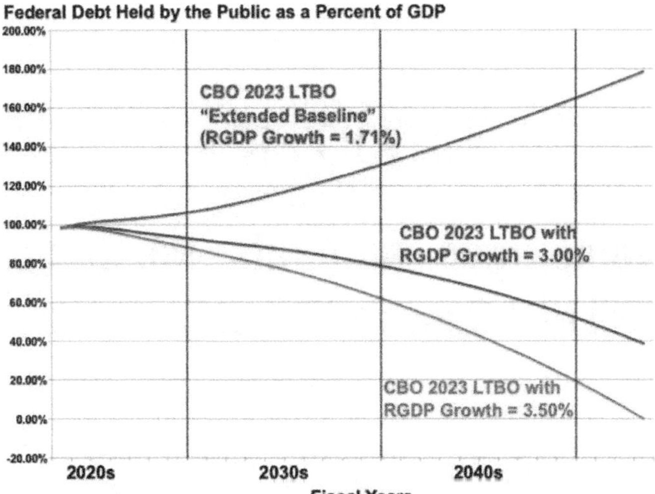
Faster Growth Will Solve Our Fiscal Problems
Federal Debt Held by the Public as a Percent of GDP
200.00%
180.00%
160.00%
140.00%
120.00%
100.00%
80.00%
60.00%
40.00%
20.00%
0.00%
-20.00%
CBO 2023 LTBO
"Extended Baseline"
(RGDP Growth = 1.71%)
CBO 2023 LTBO with
RGDP Growth = 3.00%
CBO 2023 LTBO with
RGDP Growth = 3.50%
2020s
2030s
2040s
Fiscal Years
LRW 080823
1

CHAPTER 4

Trump Trade and Tariffs—No, Trump Will NOT Cause a Global Trade War

"Expanding the United States' trade abroad can offer the advantages of competition: increased productivity, greater economic growth, increased innovation, lower prices, and more variety. New markets may not only provide domestic firms with more potential customers than are available in the local market and a chance to build economies of scale; they also offer the opportunity to purchase lower-cost inputs. Consumers—and disproportionately low-income consumers—may benefit as import competition fosters innovation and product differentiation, and drives down the prices of goods and services."

—Trump Administration's Council of Economic Advisers Report, 2018

"I use tariffs as a weapon."

That is what Donald Trump has told us nearly every time we have discussed trade with him.

He has spooked many free marketeers who believe in the virtues of free trade (and that includes us) with his talk of a 10% across the board tariff and tariff as high as 60% on China.

But this man is a very shrewd negotiator.

Who do you think is listening very intently when he makes that threat of punitive tariffs on China? President Xi and his economic advisors in Beijing. Trump is sending a warning shot at the Beijing power structure. They know that while a 60% tariff would hurt American consumers and raise prices here at home, their own struggling economy would be hit even harder by such a tax. Their economy depends on access to America's vast consumer market. Trump was in effect saying to Xi: Change your predatory trade practices or we're coming at you.

We doubt they will call his bluff.

But we outright reject the idea that Trump is a protectionist.

We will never forget a key moment in the 2016 campaign when we were traveling on the campaign plane with Trump and the team was preparing his final edits on his economic speech at the Detroit Economic Club. We were joined by Steve Mnuchin, Steven Miller, Jared Kushner, and, of course, Trump. After the lengthy discussion and myriad edits, when the speech was ready to be put in the teleprompter, Trump strolled over to us and asked, "What do you guys think of the speech?"

We looked at each other apprehensively and Larry Kudlow spoke up for the three of us. "We like it, Donald [he wasn't yet president], but we are concerned that there is nothing in here about the benefits of international trade. You need to reassure people that you understand that trade is good, and you don't want to sound like a protectionist." We braced for Trump's reaction as he thought about what we had said. Then he blurted out to everyone in the cabin: "They're right. We need to make the point that I'm not an isolationist or a protectionist." He added: "I'm a businessman. Of course I understand the value of international trade." Then he turned to Steven Miller and said: "Steve, we need to add a sentence that says free trade is good, but it needs to be fair trade. I don't want to come across as a protectionist."

Is Trump an old-fashioned protectionist?

We don't think so.

We think he is a strategic thinker on trade. By that we mean that he wants to continue to allow and encourage the freedom to trade among nations. Trump believes China is a special case in this strategy because of its predatory trade practices and its increasing threats to American and world security.

With respect to other nations, Larry Kudlow calls the Trump trade doctrine: "trade reciprocity." If you hit us with tariffs, we will hit you back. This is hardly Milton Friedman unilateral free trade, but we've seen the strategy work like a charm. Trump is an ongoing work in progress on trade. Our goal as informal economic advisors to Trump for the past eight years has always been to nudge him in the more pro-free trade direction while being respectful of the promises he made on the campaign trail of taking a tougher stance on trade deals than previous presidents. We have been excoriated over the years for supporting Trump and "selling out our free trade principles." Far from it. We always said from day one to everyone—including most importantly Trump himself—that we did not fully agree with his philosophy on trade, but we wanted to give him the best advice we could along the way.

Trump always intimated to us that he was using the threat of tariffs against China, Canada, Mexico, and the European Union, among others, "as leverage to get them to lower their tariffs on American products." His view was that persistent trade deficits with other nations were *prima facie* evidence that they were getting the better of us and that by threatening trade sanctions, he could force foreigners to buy more American steel, soybeans, pork, blue jeans, bourbon, and the like.

After spending much time with Donald Trump, we developed a pretty good understanding of his philosophy on trade and his trade negotiation tactics and goals. The good news is that he firmly supports and recognizes the advantages of trade across national borders. But he also believes the way to get there is to use America's prized multitrillion-dollar consumer market as the bargaining chip to force our competitors to open up their markets to us.

The crux of the Trump trade agenda during his presidency, and if he returns to the White House, is to "negotiate much better deals for American companies and American workers." He says that his ultimate objective is the reduction in global tariffs and trade barriers in ways that create more jobs in the United States. Because Trump is a master negotiator, he likes the idea of negotiating one-on-one bilateral trade deals, rather than complicated multilateral trade deals that don't always give the United States a strategic benefit. This view runs against the tide of trade negotiations for at least the last several decades.

We should say that we have great respect for two of Trump's longtime and continuing advisors on trade policy: Bob Lighthizer and Peter Navaro. While we didn't always agree with their strategies, we appreciated their keen knowledge of trade laws and their convictions that the president must always put America's interests first in any trade negotiations. We consider them friends and not rivals—even when we came to different strategic conclusions. They will likely play an important role in a second Trump term.

WHAT IS THE TRUMP TRADE DOCTRINE?

To understand the Trump strategy on international trade, one has to first read his best-selling book, *The Art of the Deal.* One thing we have discovered about Trump is that he's an expert on cutting the best deal possible. There were many occasions when he used the THREAT of tariffs as leverage for nations agreeing to terms that advanced American national security and economic security goals.

We have a strategic advantage over other nations. Just as we benefit from being the world reserve currency, the U.S. also has a strategic advantage because EVERY nation—particularly China—has to trade with the U.S. to have access to our multi-trillion-dollar consumer market. When it comes to trade, we are the world.

Trump recognizes and exploits this strategic advantage. We were continually impressed with his negotiating skills. His opening bids on trade have been very tough. He pulled the United States out of the Pacific trade deal, as promised. He insisted on the renegotiation of NAFTA, which resulted in a robust new agreement with enhanced protections for American manufacturers, automakers, farmers, dairy producers, and workers (more on that below). But the overall concept of North America as a free trade zone remains largely intact.

When the Europeans refused to pay their fair share of the bills for NATO, Trump threatened high tariffs on goods imported from Euroland. The Europeans didn't call his bluff. They coughed up the money. When the Mexican government refused to help secure the border, Trump threatened stiff tariffs, on Mexican products. Mexico City later agreed to help deter illegal migrants. When China was blatantly stealing the intellectual property of American firms and engaging in predatory trade practices, the threat of tariffs made Beijing cease and desist.

Trump often pointed to a 2017 analysis by the Office of the United States Trade Representative, which estimated that IP thievery perpetrated by China alone costs us between $225 billion and $600 billion each year. China also accounts for a major share of stolen U.S. trade secrets. That costs us another $180-$540 billion annually. Millions of U.S. jobs are put in jeopardy because of the unfair trade practices routinely employed by China and other countries.

The Trump doctrine on trade regarded this theft as something that cannot stand. He believed then, and believes now, that Washington tolerated these abuses out of a misguided fear that to stand up to these nations would risk overturning the apple cart of free trade. There has also been a sense of resignation in previous administrations on this issue—a conviction that there wasn't much America could do about it.

Trump's saw this as nonsense and that America had been played as a sucker. He didn't think the United States should absorb all the production and innovation costs of developing a new technology, or drug, or vaccine, and let the rest of the world copycat the invention or the patent with impunity. His solution was to impose punitive tariffs on nations that steal our technology.

Trump has often been accused of threatening to start a "trade war." But Trump's response to this is that we are already IN a trade war and we've unilaterally stopped fighting.

Trump means it when he says that "trade wars are winnable." Trump's view is that any tit-for-tat retaliation by our trading partners will hurt them far more than us.

Most nations do have higher tariffs than we do. In Trump's first term the Council of Economic Advisers pointed out that in 2017, the average tariff rate in the United States was about 3.5

percent. In Canada the rate was about 4.1 percent, in the European Union 5 percent, in South Korea 13.9 percent, in China 10 percent, in India 13 percent, and in Mexico 7 percent. The rest of the world imposes tariffs almost triple what we charge on imports. This doesn't include non-tariff barriers—quotas, domestic content rules, domestic ownership rules (prevalent in China), value-added taxes and others—that can effectively block American companies from penetrating a foreign market.

"How is this free trade?" Trump would ask us many times. His view was, "It isn't free and it certainly isn't fair trade, when we lower our trade barriers but other nations don't lower theirs."

BIDEN VERSUS TRUMP ON TARIFFS

It may surprise readers that although everyone thinks of Trump as the anti-free trader, tariffs have been higher under Biden-Harris than Trump. So how is it that Trump is the dangerous trade protectionist?

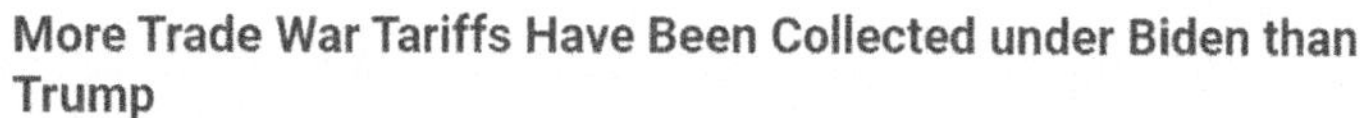

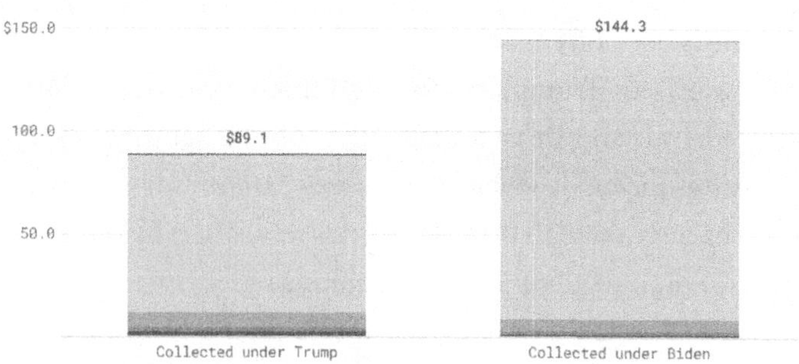

Even the Brookings Institution, a liberal Washington think tank, had to concede on the third anniversary of Trump's revised trade agreement with Mexico and Canada that it had resulted in "significant progress in expanding trade, investment, and jobs, as well as ensuring USMCA delivers outcomes that are good for workers and broader group of society across North America." The analysis went on to say,

> Trade and investment have expanded across the region, and cooperation among officials, industry, and civil society has strengthened and deepened. The USMCA dispute resolution mechanisms have been utilized, which demonstrates an investment by all governments in the rules. Furthermore, the success of the labor chapter rapid response mechanism has underscored how this new type of trade agreement can lead to material impacts on working conditions.

There were other agreements with countries such as Japan, South Korea, Brazil, and Ecuador. These agreements, pointed out the Council of Economic Advisers, went "well beyond the lower tariffs that have been the focus of past trade agreements by addressing structural and technical barriers to free and trade."[1]

DO TRADE DEFICITS MATTER?

Another pillar of the Trump trade doctrine is the view that U.S. trade deficits are a major problem for the American economy going forward. Our friend Bob Lighthizer, who ably served as

1 https://www.whitehouse.gov/wp-content/uploads/2021/07/2021-ERP.pdf

Trump Trade Representative, and will play a major role in a second Trump term, is an advocate of this philosophy.

A trade deficit occurs when the value of the products we sell to a foreign country is less than the value of what they sell us. We have discovered from personal experience that Trump views the trade deficit with nations like China, Japan, and Korea, and with the members of the European Union, as a major brake on economic growth. One of the conditions he established with these trading partners is that they must work to lower their annual surpluses with the United States. By far our biggest trade deficit is with China, which was $279 billion in 2023. But the reported trade deficit often does not include financial, computer, accounting, consulting, and other service areas that the United States usually dominates.

We've believed Trump and Lighthizer are far too concerned with the trade deficit—which is offset almost dollar for dollar by our capital import surplus. Nations run trade surpluses with the United States because they want to invest here and need surplus dollars to do so. We prepared a study for the Trump administration in early 2018 showing that economic prosperity in America has been strongly and positively correlated with trade deficits, not trade surpluses. Yes, you read that right, and do not wipe your glasses or adjust your computer screen. This finding surprised President Trump and some of his trade representatives, but the evidence is powerful:

Start with the birth of our nation. Arthur has compiled the data going back to colonial times and through the end of the Civil War. From 1747 until 1854, we ran a trade deficit virtually every year. To be exact, the United States had 95 years of trade deficits and only 13 years of trade surpluses, including 1775 and 1776 (the revolution), 1811 and 1813 (also a war), 1842, 1843, and 1844. The world's greatest economy was effectively created by importing foreign capital net, that is, by running trade deficits. By importing capital net, the United States grew enormously, employed workers at high wages, and created a job and wealth creation machine rarely seen before. America's greatest years of growth and prosperity were years of trade deficits.

It is also unquestionably true that protectionism can have very negative consequences for the United States. During the Great Depression, the volume of international trade plummeted after the passage of the infamous Smoot-Hawley tariff, which put taxes on the imports of thousands of products. As a consequence, there was not much of a trade deficit or surplus in the 1930s as the economy and living standards continued to contract. The lesson of the Great Depression is that what matters for an economy to grow is the volume of trade, not whether one country is running a trade surplus with another.

President John F. Kennedy reduced global tariffs by some 35 percent early in his presidency. From the first quarter of 1963 through the first quarter of 1966, generally viewed as the Kennedy era, six of 13 quarters had growth above a 6 percent annual rate, five quarters above 8 percent, and only three quarters slightly below 3 percent. That's amazing.

The 1970s was the last period when the United States ran persistent—though small—trade surpluses. The presidencies of Nixon, Ford, and Carter gave America the worst decade for real family incomes, the stock market, and national wealth accumulation since the Great Depression.

In the 1980s the United States cut tax rates, regulations, and inflation (by strengthening and stabilizing the dollar). Reagan was a free trade advocate. As the American economy exploded with growth, foreigners poured trillions of dollars of capital into the United States. The faster the growth, the more the trade deficit exploded as a consequence.

During the height of the Great Recession, from 2008 to 2009, the U.S. trade deficit decreased significantly, even as the unemployment rate increased from 5.8 percent to 9.3 percent. From 2009 to 2014, imports to the United States and the trade deficit increased significantly, but the U.S. unemployment rate decreased from 9.3 percent to 6.2 percent.

That's American history on trade in a nutshell: The U.S. trade deficit widens during U.S. booms (Reagan, Kennedy, and Clinton) and narrows during U.S. recessions (Nixon, Carter). During booms, investments in the United States are more attractive, and during contractions, U.S. investments are less attractive.

Will Trump Cause a Global Trade War—NO!

We are also persuaded that despite the threats of tariffs and the rejection of prior trade deals, Trump wants to get to genuine freer trade as his final goal. It didn't get much attention, but at the end of the G-7 meeting of major world leaders in Canada in June 2018, Larry, who had just been appointed National Economic Council director, pushed Trump to put on the table the option of a "zero tariff solution." This came in the wake of Trump being roundly criticized by Canada's prime minister, Justin Trudeau, and the European leaders for threatening a break from the "new world order" consensus on reducing trade barriers. Trump took Larry's advice and suggested to his counterparts: "No tariffs, no barriers. That's the way it should be. And no subsidies." Then he continued: "You want tariff free, no barriers. And you want no subsidies."

That doesn't sound like the declaration of a trade protectionist. It was illuminating that the defenders of the "new world order" in Canada rejected Trump's offer and then denounced him after he left town. This suggested that Trump might be right: the rest of the world wants American open borders for their trade but shrinks at the idea of opening up their own to American goods.

Agree or disagree with Donald Trump's stance on trade, he reset the terms of the debate. And it's revealing that the Biden Administration has largely maintained his policy toward China. That's because China hasn't been following the rules of the international trading system, and it took Donald Trump to call them on the carpet. While we're hopeful he will place less emphasis on trade deficits if he returns to the White House, we know that he's already struck a blow for trade that is freer and fairer—and that progress is a big factor in his appeal to voters throughout the country.

As far as the Trump 10 percent revenue tariff proposal, we are uneasy about this. But if the revenues gained are used to cut other income or payroll taxes that may even have a worse effect on jobs and the economy, then we think the hysteria from the Democratic economists is just that—hysteria. The volume of U.S. imports and exports increased while Trump was president until 2020 when the virus greatly hampered world trade.

Overall, we think that the fear that Trump will cause a World War III trade war is bunk. He simply wants trade deals that put America first, and that is what a president should do.

CHAPTER 5

How the Trump Boom Became a Biden/Harris Bust

When Joe Biden and Kamala Harris came into office in January of 2021, America had suffered through a year of panic, disease, government lockdowns, and economic turmoil. Had it not been for the Covid pandemic, Donald Trump was well on his way to a 40-state reelection landslide. At the start of 2020, the economy had been booming throughout the three years of Trump's presidency, with median household income up by an astounding $6,400, the poverty rate and the unemployment rate at record lows, big gains in incomes for minorities, the stock market on a blowout bull market, and the world at peace.

Covid obviously changed everything. And we are not here to defend many of the decisions Trump made in those first six months of the virus. Shutting down the economy (remember it was supposed to be "14 days to stop the spread") was a catastrophic mistake, though in our meetings with Trump in the spring of 2020, we can assure readers that Trump's highest priority was getting American businesses and schools back open and getting American workers back on the job. It is also worth noting that more Americans died from Covid during the Biden presidency than the Trump presidency.

Over the last six months of Trump's presidency—after the one-third decline in U.S. output during the lockdowns—the economy was roaring back, with a 10.9% rise in GDP. The economy was teed up for an expansion and a return to normalcy and good times thanks to the amazing success of Trump's "operation warp speed" vaccine.

A strong case could be made that all the incoming president had to do was...nothing. Let the natural healing powers of the American economy take hold.

Alas, Biden arrived in the White House and proceeded to push all the wrong buttons. The Democrats used Covid as an excuse to spend multiple trillions of dollars on welfare, income redistribution, corporate welfare programs, white elephant projects, and green energy handouts. Never before in history has one administration wasted so much money in such a short period of time.

This chapter explains how Biden—and Harris, who supported every Biden initiative and even provided the tie-breaking vote in the Senate for nearly $3 trillion of debt spending—so rapidly derailed the economy.

DROWNING IN DEBT

When Trump left office and Biden entered, Congress had already spent roughly $3 trillion on Covid-related programs. This included an unwise and unnecessary $1 trillion handout to families AFTER he lost the election.

All told the federal government spent more money on Covid under Trump and then Biden than America had spent adjusted for inflation to win World War II. At least we won THAT war.

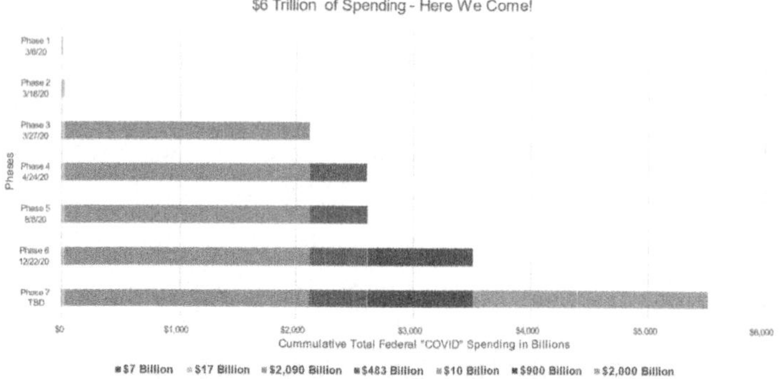

Again, Trump for sure does deserve some of the blame for this blizzard of spending.

The last thing the American economy needed was trillions of dollars more debt when the recovery was already well under way.

What was the rationale for all of the additional spending in 2021 and 2022? The truth is—especially when Biden entered office—most of the programs had nothing to do with Covid. Covid tracked the historic pattern of how Washington deals with a crisis—the federal government panics during periods of turmoil. Both parties do this. George W. Bush panicked after the 2008 financial crisis and famously said that we needed to suspend the free enterprise system "to save it." Democrats have happily seized on periods of crisis—war, terrorism, economic contraction, a pandemic—to dramatically increase spending on programs that expand the reach of government—far beyond what American voters would tolerate during normal times. This is why crises tend to have a ratcheting effect in expanding the size and scope of government, as University of Maryland economist Mancur Olson famously explained in his book, *The Rise and Decline of Nations*.

The usual excuse is that government spending is needed as an economic "stimulus" when events turn south. This was the justification for the massive tax, spend, and borrow policies of the New Deal during the Great Depression. FDR with his New Deal spending (and then taxing) spree turned what might have been a temporary financial panic into a Great Depression that lasted more than a decade, with the unemployment rate never falling below 10%. Yet most historians and history books label the New Deal a great success—when it in reality it prolonged economic misery. For more on this, we urge readers to read *Taxes Have Consequences* by Laffer, et al.

Then there was Obama's spending blowout on "shovel-ready projects" after the 2008 market crash. It carried a hefty price tag of $830 billion—an unthinkable amount at that time. But the economic recovery that followed was anemic—so much so that Obama's own numbers showed that the economy performed worse with the governmental expansion than if the spending and deficits had never happened at all. The chart below shows the similar failure of the Obama trillion spending spree.

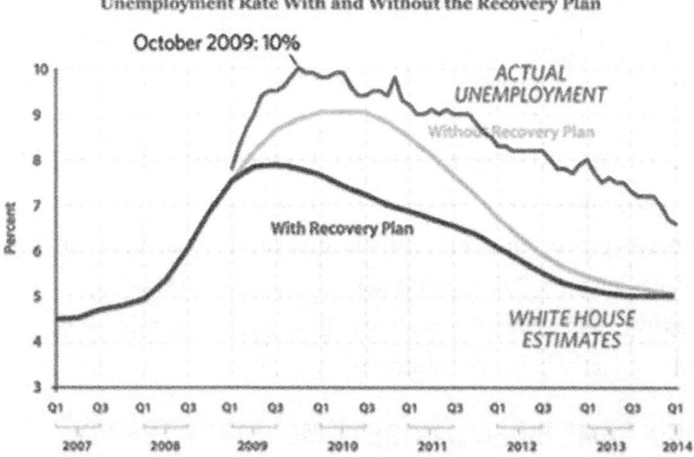

Source: "The Job Impact of the American Recovery and Reinvestment Plan," 2009, president's Council of Economic Advisers; Bureau of Labor Statistics, Labor Department. Graphic: The Heritage Foundation, April 2015.

Lest readers think we are exaggerating the extent of the Obamanomics stimulus failure: these numbers in the above chart came from the Obama administration itself. The White House's own claims when it sold Congress on the "stimulus" program shows the unemployment rate would have fallen faster and the economy more briskly had Washington not borrowed $830 billion. Now the Obama administration says that its own forecasts were wrong and that the economy turned out to be weaker than they thought. Sure.

The reasons for the feeble economy in Obama's first term can't all be blamed on the failed stimulus bill. Obamacare, the tax hikes on the rich, minimum wage increases, EPA regulations on our energy industry, and Dodd-Frank slowed growth and hiring too.

One lesson that has hopefully been learned or relearned over the past decade is that government spending on food stamps and unemployment benefits, green energy subsidies for companies like Solyndra, and transit grants for rail projects to nowhere is no way to improve economic conditions in the short term and certainly not in the medium or long term. The Congressional Budget Office tells us that the long-term effects of the stimulus plan were negative. In other words, we are a little poorer this year and every year going forward because of the massive borrowing. All we have to show for ourselves after the borrowing binge is massive debt repayments that will be made over decades. This didn't exactly help "the children."

THEN CAME BIDEN'S MODERN MONETARY THEORY

This brings us to the Biden scheme to fix an American economy that was on the mend and didn't need fixing.

Biden and his financially incompetent economic team brought to the White House a new economic theory called Modern Monetary Theory (MMT).

This was a crackpot economic strategy that came from Australian economist Bill Mitchell about a decade ago. MMT was Keynesianism on steroids. John Maynard Keynes (1883-1946) argued that government should stimulate the economy by spending and borrowing during a short-term shock like an economic crisis or a war, then pull back to a reasonable level of spending and debt once the crisis has passed.

Under MMT, the crisis never ends and there is no reason to stop borrowing and spending. Proponents posit that because the dollar is the world's reserve currency and the Treasury can sell bonds at low interest rates, Uncle Sam can spend and borrow limitlessly with no economic risk. As Stephanie Kelton, an economist at SUNY Stony Brook, put it: "Deficits can help us fight a myriad of problems that plague our economy—inequality, poverty and unemployment, climate change, housing, health care, and more."

Free-market economists scoffed. History is awash with nations that tried to spend and borrow their way to prosperity: ancient Rome, interwar Germany, Argentina, postwar Britain, and more recently Bolivia, Mexico, Zimbabwe, Greece, and Venezuela. It never worked—not even once.

But on the left, MMT caught on as a convenient fad explanation for why Barack Obama's $800 billion stimulus plan in 2009 failed to lift the economy out of its ditch and failed to yield anything like the promised 4% annual growth that we were promised. The MMT crowd explained the spending wasn't enough. Obama was too thrifty! That became a common chant from New

York Times columnist and Nobel Prize winner Paul Krugman and it caught on.

In 2020, the Democratic Party en masse fully embraced MMT. Pitifully, every Democrat in Congress lined up and drank the Kool-Aid. The above-mentioned Ms. Kelton served as a top economic adviser to Sen. Bernie Sanders, runner-up for the party's nomination, and later co-authored a report for the Biden campaign that served as a blueprint for its spending blowout.[2] In 2021, MMT gave the administration and Democratic lawmakers an academic imprimatur for what was to become an avalanche of debt-financed spending, four times as large as Mr. Obama's stimulus 12 years earlier.

This is the short story version of how Biden and Kamala persuaded Congress to shovel $4 trillion more into social-welfare programs, corporate-welfare grants, leftist environmental programs, college and healthcare subsidies and more. In a testament to MMT's sway, 17 Nobel economics laureates signed a 2021 statement asserting that all this spending "will ease longer-term inflationary pressures." They advised Biden to "go big" on his spending ambitions.[3]

You can see why politicians—especially on the left of the political spectrum—would be attracted to this sophistry. Mr. Biden and the MMT crowd crowed that they had invented a perpetual-motion machine. Congress could borrow off the federal credit card and still feel good about itself in the morning. Nothing bad would happen.

---

2 https://joebiden.com/wp-content/uploads/2020/08/UNITY-TASK-FORCE-RECOMMENDATIONS.pdf

3 https://www.epi.org/open-letter-from-nobel-laureates-in-support-of-economic-recovery-agenda/

Or so they thought. Instead, they unleashed the worst inflation in 40 years.

Average weekly earnings of employees rose 15% between January 2021 and May 2024. But that was a loss in real terms, since prices were up 19%. Even with trillions in handouts, working Americans saw their average real annual income decline by more than $2,300 in today's dollars during Biden's first three years in office. To our knowledge, not one of those Nobel economists has issued a retraction. Worse, in June of 2024 these same economists who had endorsed MMT swore on the pages of the *New York Times* that the chance of a rush of inflation was "remote." But the country ended up saddled with the biggest bulge in prices since the Jimmy Carter era.

FISCAL PYROMANIACS

What's frightening is that at the time of this writing, we've only felt the first minor ripple effects of the financial damage done to our country. It is as if our country was run by swindler Bernie Madoff—who lived high on the hog until the fraud was discovered. Bills come due. Debts must be repaid. It may be a decade or two before the United States recovers from the fiscal damage inflicted by Bidenomics. The June 2024 Congressional Budget Office fiscal analysis of our nation's finances is full of fiscal doom and gloom and serves as an epitaph to the gross financial mismanagement of the Biden era. The chart below shows we are quickly tapping out on the federal credit card—if we haven't already.

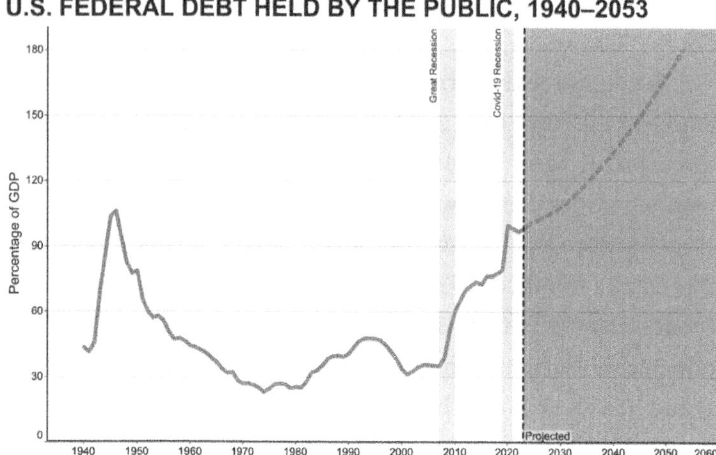

In fairness to Biden, the fiscal outlook was miserable when he came into office following the Covid economic crash. But Biden's unforgivable sin was taking over a fiscal situation in turmoil and figuratively pouring gasoline on the fire.

It's been four years of multi-trillion-dollar spending bills, deficits of between $1.5 and $2 trillion a year, a 20% rise in the price level, and falling real incomes. Trump was no fiscal tightwad either, but this is the wreckage of MMT put into practice.

The June 2024 CBO report served as a blaring ambulance siren of what happens if we stay on the Bidenomics track. Here are the unhappy lowlights:

- Budget deficits of an average of nearly $2 trillion a year for the next four years at least. There's no pretense of bending this curve down.
- The national debt hits $50 trillion in 10 years
- The annual federal budget reaches $10 trillion in 10 years

- Revenues NEVER catch up with the spending even if the Trump tax cuts are allowed to expire—as Biden has promised.

We wonder if communist spies from Beijing were to break into the White House and concocted a master plan to sabotage the American economy whether they could come up with a better plan than this one.

We know that some of our Democratic friends will object that Republicans have run up massive amounts of red ink themselves. And that is true. The debt grew under Reagan, both Bush presidencies, and under Trump. We are not cheerleaders for Republicans and freely that the out-of-control-spending in Washington is a BIPARTISAN.

But what's different about the Biden spending blitz is that we have nothing of long- term benefit to show from it. Under Reagan, the deficit went up. But most of that money was used for two purposes: first, to finance tax rate reductions that super-charged the economy and helped unleash a two-decade long boom; and second, to rebuild the American military to win the Cold War and defeat the Soviet Union (the "evil empire," as Reagan called it). Our children and grandchildren will bear some of the burden of paying off that debt, much like the baby boomers paid off the debts from saving the world from tyranny during World War II. Trump's deficits mostly financed pro-growth tax cuts and management of the Covid crisis.

Nothing that Biden has spent money on has benefited the overall health of the economy or the future of the planet. Biden has amazingly racked up trillions of dollars of new debt while at the same time neutering our military and depleting our resource reserves. As we showed in a previous chapter, the Green New Deal financed another round of failed and bankrupt green energy boondoggles.

HOW BIDEN-HARRIS MORPHED INTO JIMMY CARTER

If the chronic fatigue syndrome we as a nation are living through now is starting to feel familiar, it's because those over the age of 50 will recall those malaise years of the 1970s. For those younger and who don't remember, under part-time President Jerry Ford and then much more so under the hapless Jimmy Carter, the decade of the 1970s was one seemingly endless nightmare of economic turmoil and national security setback after another.

The witches brew of high inflation of 7 to 10 percent by 1979 and ever-increasing tax rates, which rose as high as 70%, capsized the economy. The stock market, for example, lost more than 50% of its value adjusted for inflation. Real family incomes cratered under Carter because inflation rose so much faster than family take-home pay. Interest rates soared and homes became unaffordable. Gas prices tripled. Carter blamed "big oil" and "invested" in pipe dream green energy alternatives, all of which went bankrupt.

Every time inflation rose, the economic whiz kids in Washington assured us the high prices were just temporary. (Unlike Biden, they didn't use the term "transitory.") When prices kept rising, Carter blamed corporate greed and installed price controls and windfall profits taxes, which only made problems worse. Carter had the worst record on inflation in modern times. Biden is right behind him, as shown in the chart on the next page.

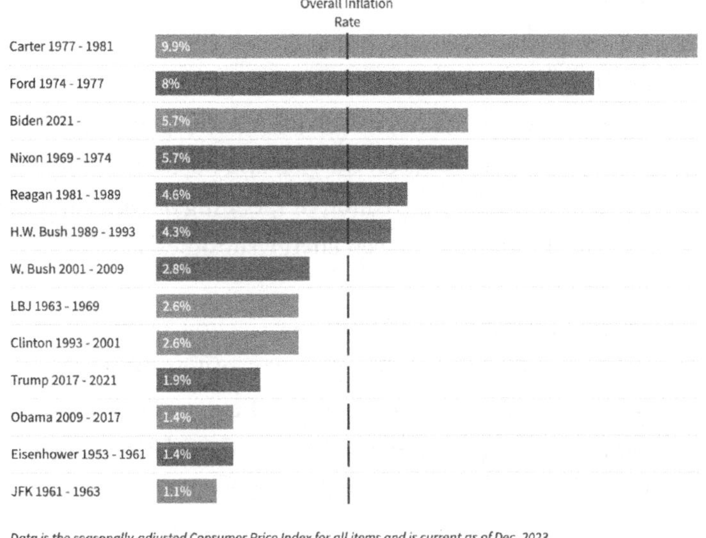

Because America was so weak at home in the 1970s, our enemies abroad capitalized. Soviet tanks rolled into Afghanistan and troops into Nicaragua, while Iran held dozens of Americans hostage for more than a year.

Federal spending and debt also soared and the private sector started shrinking.

Carter's response to the leaky faucet of bad news was to point at the American people and lecture us to turn down the thermostat, put on a sweater, and learn to live with less. (But even Carter didn't threaten to abolish air conditioning and gas heat.)

Interest rates on mortgages skyrocketed to 17% and buying a home became financially out of reach for the majority of Americans.

The new term that slid into the American lexicon was "stagflation." This was the combination of high prices and sluggish economic growth.

Does any of this sound familiar?

Intentionally or not, Biden and Harris started calling for policies that were straight out of the Carter playbook. More price controls, higher taxes on the rich and businesses, breaking up big business, another $2 trillion in spending on programs like student loan "forgiveness," green energy subsidies, and mortgage relief programs.

Just as with Jimmy Carter in the election of1980, Kamala Harris is now offering a policy platform of four more years of Americans making larger financial sacrifices, while government expands in size, scope and intrusiveness. That platform won the incumbent Jimmy Carter 41% of the vote in 1980.

BIDEN'S WAR ON ENERGY

In addition to runaway federal spending, Biden and Harris also brought to the White House a pledge to destroy America's fossil fuel industry. His first act as president was to kill the Keystone XL pipeline and he has used all his bureaucratic resources to try to stymie the American oil, gas, and coal industries. It's the primary reason that gas prices soared from $2.49 a gallon under Trump to between $3.50 and $4.50 a gallon (and above $5 a gallon in California) under Biden.

The Institute for Energy Research has chronicled dozens of actions and orders by the Biden administration that have blocked or created financial disincentives for drilling.[4] These include taking hundreds of thousands of acres offline for drill-

4 https://www.instituteforenergyresearch.org/fossil-fuels/chronology-of-bidens-gasoline-price-hike/

ing, canceling pipelines, and imposing restrictive environmental regulations that make drilling more expensive. He blames major oil companies for high gas prices rather than his own policies.

And despite President Biden's best efforts, the U.S. is, as Biden has put it: "approaching record levels of oil and natural gas production."

But this is only because the price of oil has skyrocketed from $50 a barrel to as high $90 a barrel under Biden.

This was a reversal of course from Trump's pro-drilling policies. By 2019, we had achieved Trump's goal of energy independence. That is to say, the U.S. was a net EXPORTER of oil, gas, and coal.[5] The Energy Information Agency had predicted that the U.S. could produce as much as 15 million barrels of oil under current trends.

A study by the group the two of us co-founded, Unleash Prosperity, finds that under Biden energy policies the U.S. has produced roughly 2.5 billion FEWER barrels of oil than would have been the case under Trump. This is the equivalent of roughly 3 to 5 million barrels a day lost from production. In other words, the U.S. has lost roughly $200 million A DAY, which amounts to more than $250 billion of lost output during the Biden presidency.

This has done nothing to reduce greenhouse gas emissions. Instead of the oil, gas, and coal coming from the U.S., a larger share now comes from Russia, Iran and OPEC nations.

---

5 https://www.eia.gov/todayinenergy/detail.php?id=43395

Figure 4. Expected oil production for 2023, by source of productivity estimate

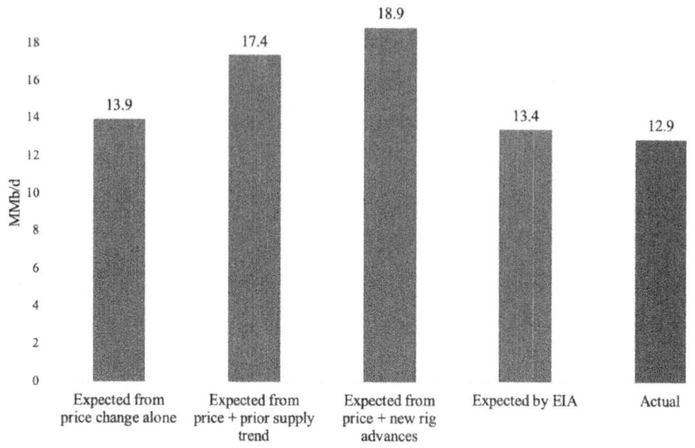

	Expected from price change alone	Expected from price + prior supply trend	Expected from price + new rig advances	Expected by EIA	Actual
MMb/d	13.9	17.4	18.9	13.4	12.9

Sources: U.S. EIA monthly data through December 2023.
Note: Expectations are as of early 2021 for a period, such as Jan-Dec 2023, where oil prices are $65 per barrel in 2019 prices.

Meanwhile, Kamala Harris has endorsed AOC's radical green new deal and has called for a ban on all oil and gas fracking. Most of our energy production today comes from shale oil and gas, which we gain access to through the fracking process. To be against fracking is like being against a cure for cancer.

STUDENT LOAN BAILOUTS WILL COST TAXPAYERS $160 BILLION+

One of Joe Biden's most outrageous and unjust policies has been the "forgiveness" of student loans. More than 40 million borrowers owe a total of $1.77 trillion in loans, according to the Federal Reserve—which is mostly a result of the hyper-inflation of college tuitions that have driven annual college costs to near $100,000 a year at some elite universities.

Biden has already forgiven $160 billion of loans that were taken out by almost five million borrowers. It has never been clear why noncollege graduates should have to pay for those who did attend college but won't pay their loans back. It has also never been made clear why taxpayers rather than the universities should be on the hook for these unpaid debts.

The latest Biden-Harris plan forces taxpayers to cover the full cost of college except for monthly payments capped at a maximum of 5 percent of income above 225 percent of the federal poverty level, which is $67,500 for a family of four.

Over a million student loan borrowers would pay zero according to Biden's own estimate.

The Biden administration says the plan will cost taxpayers $138 billion, while the Penn-Wharton budget model's median estimate is that it will cost taxpayers $475 billion over the 10-year budget window. That's another half-trillion-dollar inflation bomb.

We believe this is all just a ploy to eventually make college free to students. That means taxpayers pick up the tab for university spending, something Kamala favors. This comes at a time when some universities are now charging $90,000 a year for the college experience. This will mean that the ivory-towered colleges that have charged families outrageous increases in tuitions, now will have no restraints whatsoever and with this new plan, universities will soon be charging $100,000 a year or more.

UNDER BIDEN-HARRIS GOVERNMENT IS THE FASTEST GROWING INDUSTRY

One area where Biden has performed well—until recently—has been keeping the unemployment rate low. Much of this is due to a decline in labor force participation, as the federal government continues to pay welfare benefits to those who don't work.

But as we have noted previously, the biggest increase in employment in the last two years under Biden has been government. Public payrolls since Biden came into office have swelled by an astonishing 1.7 million net hires. Health care, which is half government, half private, is up 1.65 million.

By contrast, under Trump, ALL of the net new jobs were outside of government and health care. Government employment actually shrank during Trump's first term, mostly due to reductions in hiring at the state and local level.

We still can't figure out why—given the $2 trillion federal deficit and the tens of billions of dollars of unfunded state and local pension liabilities—states, localities and feds keep adding to their payrolls.

Under Biden and Harris health care employment grew four times faster than under Trump and government employment surged whereas public sector hiring FELL under Trump.

BIDEN LOVES BIG GOVERNMENT

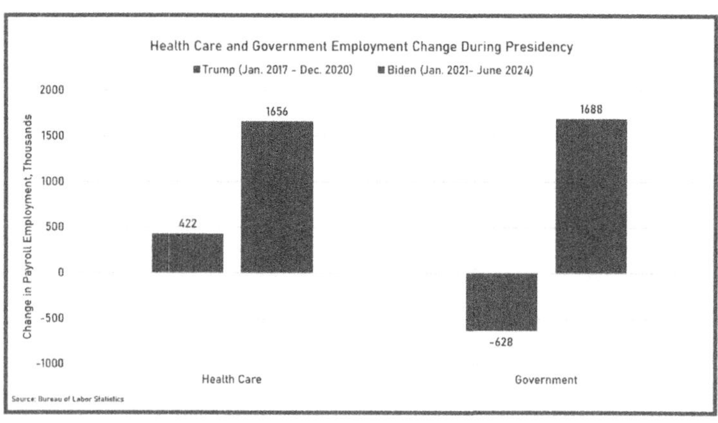

Even these numbers distort the disproportionate impact government is exerting on the economy. That's because under the Biden administration, Congress has appropriated hundreds of billions of dollars in corporate welfare subsidies. For example, the Chips Act and the misnamed Inflation Reduction Act funneled tens of billions of dollars to the microchip industry, green energy, and electric cars.

Government is thus adding hundreds of thousands of private sector jobs that are primarily financed by taxpayers. This is a losing proposition. The only way the government can spend money to pay for these jobs programs is to subtract investment and jobs from other private employers that don't have most favorable industry status from politicians. We should have learned from the Obama years that government subsidies to industries in the end leads to low-productivity spending and bankruptcies. Remember Solyndra and Fisker?

TIME TO THROW BIDENOMICS INTO THE DUSTBIN OF HISTORY

President Biden used to cite "Bidenomics" as a point of pride. Not so much anymore. It turns out most Americans are turned off by this term—and for good reason. The policies are a flop and working-class Americans, as well as retirees, know it and feel it when they struggle to pay the bills.

What a reversal of fortune from when Trump was president.

Here's an example of the superiority of the Trump record. First, while Trump was president the inflation rate averaged just a bit over 2% and the month he left office it had fallen to 1.6%—one of the lowest rates in 40 years.

Then Biden comes into office with his $5 trillion spend, borrow, and print money program. Within 18 months, the inflation rate had zoomed up to 9.1%. How do you screw up the economy that quickly? Was he trying to ruin the American economy? Was he trying to emulate Jimmy Carter? Mercifully, the inflation rate has started to recede since the end of 2022, but the latest Bureau of Labor Statistics numbers indicate we are headed back to 4.5%—or more.

Overall consumer prices are up roughly 20% since Biden took the White House. But the necessities continue to rise much faster than that—as anyone who buys groceries, goes to the gas pump, or writes monthly bills knows.

For those trying to afford to buy a new home, the costs are even more explosive. The average payment on a 30-year mortgage payment was about $2,000 a month under Trump. Now it is closer to $3,000 a month. This is nearly a 50% price hike. Why? Because the mortgage interest rate has spiked to 7.1% nationally from 3% in 2020.

Then, of course, there is the calamity of our national debt. It's increased about $6 trillion in Biden's first three and a half years of office. Even Biden admits that if he is reelected we will borrow $1 trillion a year for the next decade He doesn't even PRETEND to have a plan to get near a balanced budget.

All of this is already causing an extreme affordability crisis for working class families and retirees on a fixed income.

More Americans than ever are going into debt to pay their bills thanks to Biden policies. In early 2024, credit card bills surpassed $1 trillion for the first time ever. Delinquencies on credit card payments are starting to rise because parents don't have the money to pay the escalating bills.

The question that Trump will be asking Americans as the election approaches is this: Are you better off than you were four years ago? The answer is crystal clear. Under Trump, median income after inflation rose by $6,000. Under Biden the average family has LOST $2,000 of real take home pay.

Then we have the government debt burden, which now stands at $31.8 trillion. Why are we borrowing such huge sums even though the Covid crisis ended two years ago? That debt burden is expected to rise to $50 trillion in 10 years even though the White House and Congress are pretending that they cut the debt. Over just the last 12 months, federal borrowing exceeded $2 trillion. This isn't progress.

As for economic growth, there isn't much. Over the past six quarters, the U.S. economy has limped along at less than 1.5% growth—half the growth rate we should be seeing in the post-COVID era.

As we show later in this book, if you think Biden was an epic failure, wait to you get a load of the Kamala express.

CHAPTER 6

Trumponomics 2.0: 17 Steps to Jump Start the U.S. Economy

In this book we've well-documented two truths: first, Trump's economic policies as president were highly successful. And second, the left-driven agenda of Joe Biden and Kamala Harris has done great damage to the prosperity of the American people and four more years of these policies could be irreversibly harmful.

Now we come to the final and perhaps most consequential chapter of the book: the Trump game plan for his second term priority of rebuilding the American economy so that it works for all Americans—not just those elites in the ruling class in Washington.

During Donald Trump's first run for President, we were constantly asked some version of the same question: What is Trumponomics all about? Does it have any cohesive theme? What are the ways Trump intends to "make America great again?"

Now we're asked, what will a Trump second term look like? What policies and priorities will Trump emphasize if he wins again?

When we asked Trump that question in the Spring of 2024, as he was sitting in his office on the second floor at Mar-a-Lago, he replied without hesitation: "Our strategy on the economy is to always put America first." Then he added: "I don't think Biden ever does that. Do you?" On policy, "I want to make sure that all the policies are oriented toward helping the middle class. They're the ones who've gotten screwed by Biden's inflation." Then he added, "we did a lot to help the U.S. corporations compete in the first term, my emphasis will be small businesses this time." He continued: "We will be very tough on China, I assure you of that."

We asked him, "What can you do right out of the gate, to rev up the economy?" His response was classic Trump: "I will have a stack of paper two inches thick on my desk when I am back in the Oval Office, and the first thing I'll do is sign hundreds of Executive Orders reversing Biden's regulatory assault on business." Then he thought about it some more and said: "And don't forget drill baby, drill. That's a high priority. Get the permits done. Build the pipelines. Refill the strategic petroleum reserve. We have more energy than any country. We should be using it. Every single drop—including clean coal. We will get back out of the crazy Paris Climate Accord, I assure you of that."

Trump is a problem solver.

He's rewritten the book on Republican orthodoxy. Some say for better. Some of the Never Trumpers in the GOP—for example, the Mitt Romney crowd—say for worse. We say mostly for better.

While he has been steadfast in his support for lower tax rates and less regulation, he broke with Republican orthodoxy on trade, foreign policy, and some regulation. He replaced two decades of stale Republican dogma with a freshly minted populist agenda. It was shocking how many millions of independent and Republican voters—and even some populist Democrats who were Bernie Sanders supporters—found Trump's approach to economic policy refreshingly attractive or at least worth a try. That's what got him elected in 2016 and almost certainly would have got him re-elected four years later had the manufactured Covid crisis not upended daily life.

He's conservative by nature, not by philosophy. His attention to detail is extraordinary. He borders on being obsessive-compulsive about all things being done exactly the right way. No mistakes. He doesn't tolerate blotches or blunders—which may be why the term that made him famous is, "You're fired!"

His attention to detail is so profound that his business associates tell the story of how he would go through any newly-constructed building or hotel that he owns and double check the condition of every room, including the comfort of the beds and the calking in the showers. Even after being elected president, at Mar-a-Lago and Bedminster he would be the first person up in the morning, checking that the hedges were cut evenly. When he plays golf at clubs he owns, he is continually tending to the course, to keep them in tip-top condition.

He's the ideal person to clean up the mess of Bidenomics.

THE MAN AND THE MESSAGE

Before we describe the principles of Trumponomics 2.0, it is critical to point out that this "populist" agenda—he likes calling it "popularism"—couldn't have been pulled off by just anyone. The message requires the right messenger. What makes Trumponomics sell is a brilliant salesman. Trump is arguably the greatest marketer of modern times—and he's taken his successes in the business world and laid them over the domain of politics.

His success in business is even more so the key to his success in politics.

What made Trump such a natural and believable messenger was that he never hid his wealth and success—instead, he wore it as a badge of honor and even flaunted it. He donned beautifully tailored suits. He drove around in limos, hung out in swanky resorts, flew around in his own plane, and built tall buildings. He boasted about his success (many times excessively) with a bravado that was appealing to millions of his voters.

Just as in 2016, he isn't running only as an outsider but as the un-politician.

Trump talks like a real person at a sports bar or a neighborhood party (we won't say like men in a locker room), not someone programmed with a teleprompter. We spent the evening with him during his Super Bowl party in February 2024 with about 250 other folks. He spent the whole evening chatting with his friends and family in a way that was genuine—not phony or pretentious.

One time we visited Trump at his compound in Bedminster on a Monday. The country club was closed. The pool is opened on Mondays to the workers at the Club and their family members. After our meeting, he walked us out and said he wanted to say hello to the parents and the kids swimming in the pool. Most of them were Hispanics extremely excited to see the President. Trump waved at the families and patiently took some photos. And this a busy guy—the former and future leader of the free world.

We have been present for several moments like this, which has only confirmed our belief that Donald Trump LOVES people and genuinely cares about the middle class. His mission—whether you agree with his policies or not—is to help them improve their lives. Many criticisms of Trump are legitimate. But we've never believed for one minute that he is in this to further enrich wealthy people like himself. He was already rich.

THE PRINCIPLES OF TRUMP POPULISM

Trumponomics revolves around a handful of core principles, all of which were on display throughout the Trump presidency.

First, always put America first. Reject globalism. The left snubbed its nose at this idea as outdated "nationalism." Wrong. The entire basis of our nation is self-government and consent of the governed. World government and multinational governing bodies, such as the World Trade Organization and the World Health Organization (which shamefully covered up for China's misdeeds related to the spread of the coronavirus), are dangerous and misguided solutions. Globalism is out. National greatness is in.

Second, focus on restoring and advancing American patriotism. Trumponomics is predicated on the core belief in the fundamental greatness and goodness of America. America is a special place, and Trump believes that to his core.

Third, empower Americans to make decisions for themselves. This is a rejection of government paternalism. Relying on the forces of competition and choice will foster better outcomes than rules, regulations, and mandates. People can decide for themselves.

The left has adopted the opposite philosophy: people aren't qualified to make their own decisions about healthcare plans, or schools, or pension investing. His passion is to empower millions more minority parents with more options for educating their kids. The left believes that poor parents would make poor choices and that competition would hurt public schools in inner cities—as if they could possibly be any worse.

Fourth, rebuild America's inner cities. This means eradicating crime, violence, drug abuse, corruption, and joblessness. Throughout his presidency, Trump told the American people the truth about liberal governance and how it had failed to keep its promises of helping the poor and distressed communities. He famously asked inner-city audiences—mostly minorities: What have the Democrats in the inner cities done for you and your neighborhoods? The answer was nothing. He also signed criminal justice legislation that eliminated lengthy criminal sentences for nonviolent offenders, while expanding access to rehabilitative programs.

Fifth, secure and protect our borders from drug runners, terrorists, illegal immigrants, and criminals. A nation without borders, Trump said many times, is not a nation. The left's response was sanctuary cities, and charges of racism and xenophobia. The public was with Trump—and they remain so solidly. The Biden Administration's attempt to take an open borders approach to immigration has resulted in a massive surge of some 6-10 million illegal migrants into the country. Even the leadership of liberal cities like New York has turned against the Biden open border policy.

Sixth, promote and support American business. Donald Trump is an unapologetically pro-business president—and he prioritized deregulating the economy so that businesses could focus their energies on maximizing profits and not trying to curry favor with government officials. The modern Democratic Party, by contrast, has become reflexively anti-business, in part because of its preoccupation with income inequality. Liberals love jobs, but they hate job creators. As Trump likes to say: you can't have one without the other.

Seventh, reject identity politics. The prevailing liberal mindset is that Americans are inherently divided by race, sexual orientation, ethnicity, and class and that there is a zero-sum game being played among all those divisions. Trumponomics starts from the premise that we are one nation under God, indivisible, and one person's gain does not come at the expense of another person. All Americans should be treated as individuals, not members of a class, and should be treated equally under the law regardless of their race, gender, and income status. It's striking how much liberals have rejected this idea and accept—if not encourage—blatant discrimination in college admissions against whites but also Asian-Americans, simply because they have higher incomes than other groups.

Eighth, reject declinism and celebrate that America's best days lie ahead. This means rejecting the limits to growth, secular stagnation, and the apocalyptic predictions about the environment that animate the left today. Trumponomics is predicated on a faith in the future and a confidence that America can solve any problem through innovation, invention, technology, and a healthy dose of just plain American can-doism. The solutions to the social, economic, and environmental threats and challenges that will confront our society in the future—from poverty to addiction to cancer—are solvable in the next generation, if not sooner.

Ninth, embrace America's most valuable role in the global economy: to lead by example. Our greatest gift to the world is to export the virtues of democratic capitalism and free enterprise. When we get it right, the rest of the world follows.

The spread of freedom and economic liberalism across the globe in the 1980s and 1990s happened in no small part because nations started to emulate the Reaganomics formula for growth. When we cut taxes, the world started cutting taxes. When we deregulated and privatized, the world followed our lead. When we stabilized and strengthened the dollar, other nations got control of inflation as well—many times by linking to the dollar.

Trump is right that the best way to promote prosperity abroad is to fix America's problems first. Then we can serve as a beacon of freedom and opportunity for nations around the globe. If we lead, the rest of the world will follow.

FINALLY, NEARLY ALL PROBLEMS CAN BE SOLVED WITH ECONOMIC GROWTH

The most important principle of Trumponomics, and the key to restoring American prosperity, is this: higher rates of economic growth. Because these higher rates will make it possible to remedy much of what ails the country, and allow Americans to live longer and happier lives.

While the left is more obsessed with income inequality—the way the economic pie is divided—Trump's view is the bigger pie gives everyone a bigger slice. Our view is that a more prosperous and financially secure nation is better for everyone—including the 100-million-plus Americans who own stock through pension and 401(k) plans.

One underappreciated dividend from this higher permanent pedestal of economic growth is that it will help address the long-term funding crisis of Social Security and Medicare. With 3 percent economic growth, up from the 1.8 percent predicted by the Social Security and Medicare actuaries, the compounding effect over 50 years means more than $50 trillion of revenues into the Medicare and Social Security trust funds, largely dissolving the funding shortfalls of these programs—and perhaps leaving them in long-term surplus, not deficit.

WHAT WILL TRUMPONOMICS 2.0 LOOK LIKE?

Now we have to address the issue: How do these principles translate into real-world policy solutions for his second term? What follows are summaries of Trump's top policy priorities—with descriptions of what he achieved in these areas while President. And there's more to come in all of these areas if he returns to the White House.

1. Slash Job Killing and Costly Regulations

The regulatory state is a $2 trillion tax on the American economy. We all want worker safety, a clean environment, and consumer protections, but in too many cases the costs of regulations far outweigh the societal benefits. Rolling back unnecessarily burdensome regulations means lower costs to businesses and consumers. As we described in chapter 2, the regulatory beast had become one of the greatest deterrents to investment here in America and a faster pace of job creation. And the Trump Administration eliminated eight regulations for every one they added. The economic impact of the Trump deregulation agenda was enormous, putting an extra $3,100 into the pocket of the average American household each year.

2. Make the Trump Tax Cuts Permanent

Lower tax rates—as JFK, Reagan, and others have proven throughout history—lead to more growth, more investment, and more jobs. Trump always saw this through the lens of American competitiveness. "We have put our businesses in a deep hole. I want us to have the tax advantage, and for America to go from worst to first on tax competitiveness." That was why he signed into law a $3.2 trillion tax relief measure. It meant that a typical family of four earning $75,000 a year saw their tax bill fall by half—a benefit valued at more than $2,000. And the corporate tax rate fell from 35 percent—the highest in the world—to 21 percent.

Trump has promised to make all of these tax cuts permanent. Why? Because they worked almost exactly as how we anticipated they would. The lower corporate tax rate and the lower rate in repatriated investment capital brought between $1 and $2 trillion back to these shores, where it was reinvested in American start-up businesses, jobs, and factories.

The Trump tax cuts also led to the rich paying MORE TAXES, as a share of all taxes paid, not less. That has been the case with every major tax cut of the last forty years.

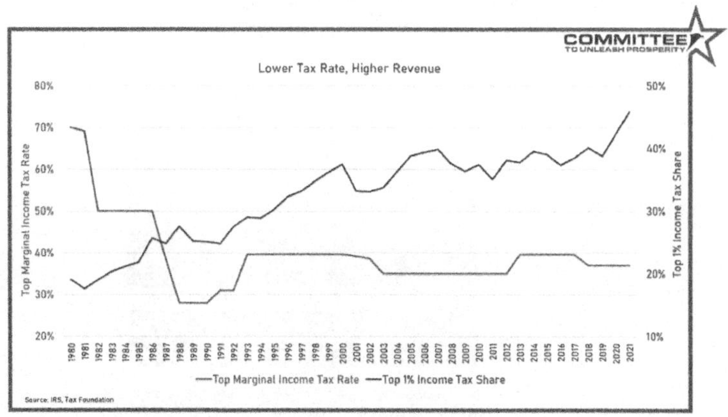

3. Replace Welfare with Work

Growth will require more able-bodied Americans getting off welfare and into jobs. Although the labor pool is aging, we are also seeing people who could be working but are staying home. The labor force participation rate in March 2024 was just 62.7 percent. That's down from 66 percent 20 years earlier.[6] There are complex reasons for this, but a key contributor is that welfare payments can often exceed in generosity the take-home pay from most starter jobs—and that isn't fair to those who do work for low wages, for taxpayers, or for the long-term economic mobility of those who could be working. Welfare—which includes cash assistance, public housing, food stamps, disability payments, unemployment benefits, and Medicaid—needs to be a hand up, not a handout.

While many leftist sociologists and other academicians may disagree with this philosophy, the good news is that most Americans of both parties agree with the Trump position.

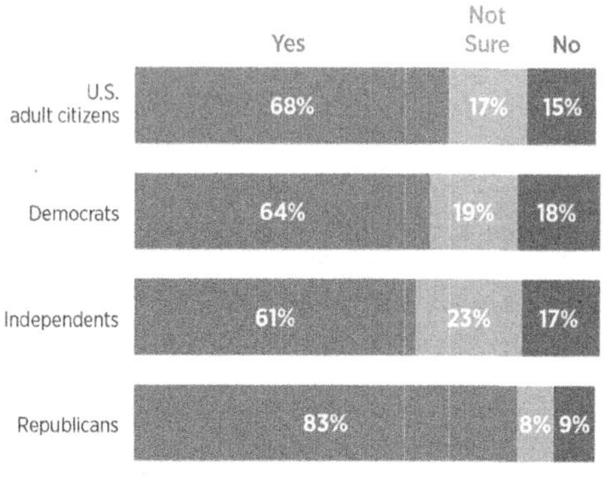

6 https://www.bls.gov/charts/employment-situation/civilian-labor-force-participation-rate.htm

4. Use America's Abundant Natural Resources

America has well more than $50 trillion of natural resources that are accessible with existing drilling and mining technologies. This is a vast storehouse of wealth that far surpasses what any other nation is endowed with. We are not running out of these resources, and the technology to discover them and put them to use for American industry and consumers—such as fracking and horizontal drilling—continues to improve rapidly over time, which means these resources are for all intents and purposes inexhaustible. We can access hundreds of years' worth of these resources—minerals, rare earth metals, oil, gas, coal, timber—with existing technology.

Using our natural resources enriches the United States in every way. It increases our national output by tens of trillions of dollars over time; it raises trillions of dollars of income tax revenues and lease and royalty payments—for the federal government and the states; it enhances our national security by making us less dependent on the Middle East, Russia, China, and other bad actors across the globe; and it can create millions of high-paying jobs for American workers. The left's philosophy is "keep it in the ground," while ours is drill, mine, and recover resources to help make the United States the world's preeminent natural resource powerhouse.

During the Trump years, the United States became a net energy exporter for the first time in 70 years and produced more oil and natural gas than any country in the world. We also became a net natural gas exporter, with an export capacity of nearly 10 billion cubic feet per day.

5. Cut Medical Costs By Demanding Health Care Price Transparency

No modern policy failure highlights the failure of one-size-fits-all government policy more than Obamacare. It denies patients the ability to tap into two forces that work to improve products and lower costs in other industries: choice and competition. Predictably, health care spending has exploded to rise since Obamacare was enacted, with pharmaceutical companies charging astronomical prices. We should call it the "Unaffordable Care Act."

The two areas of the economy that have seem massive increases in inflation have been health care and education. These also happen to be the two industries that are MOST controlled by government. We subsidize health care and education to make them "more affordable," but just the opposite has happened.

One of many ways to bring health care costs down to consumers (and to the federal government, which pays half the costs) is to require that hospitals, pharmacies, doctors, health clinics list prices for what they are charging. The Committee to Unleash Prosperity estimates that $1 to $2 trillion could be reduced from health care costs with no reduction in the quality of care, by allowing consumers to shop around for the best price—just as we do when we buy groceries, a home, a car, or a vacation. Especially in the internet era, when prices can be compared with a few clicks on a keyboard, 21st century health care should involve comparison shopping. This will foster free-market competition and lower prices.

6. Modernize America's Infrastructure

Trump focused on leveraging private and state dollars to rebuild our traditional public infrastructure—including roads, bridges, schools, airports, and ports.

We often advised him that America's most important infrastructure needs are private—factories, warehouses, research centers, office complexes, laboratories, and so on. Those were largely incentivized by the Trump tax cut and the immediate capital expensing of improvements to these facilities that are privately owned and operated. Looking ahead, we also need 21st century infrastructure that is public in benefit, but can and should be privately operated. We are talking about pipelines, liquefied natural gas (LNG) terminals, energy refineries, airports, the electric grid system, broadband development, satellites, space rockets, and so on. By simply deregulating these areas, Trump envisions a future with American investment exploding, and very little in taxpayer dollars would be needed. Look at what Space X is doing with private rocket launches as a prototype for what the private sector can do in infrastructure in dozens of other areas.

Trump is also committed to ending "infrastructure" spending that has a very low rate of return or is a money burning machine. This includes the $7 billion California high-speed rail project, most urban transit subsidies with record low numbers of passengers, and wind and solar energy projects that almost always wind up in bankruptcy.

7. Allow Every Parent in America—Regardless of Income or Skin Color—to Have Access to the Best Schools Including Private, Catholic, and Charter Schools

Test scores in America have been plummeting. Kids are graduating from high school—if at all—without even being to read the diploma. America no longer ranks in the top ten in many academic achievement ratings. Democrats cater to the teacher unions, not the children.

This is a national security and economic security crisis. It is putting our children at disadvantage when they try to compete against better educated kids from China, Japan, Europe, India, and other nations in the decades to come.

Our outmoded education model is driven by monopolistic structures that are costly, bureaucratic, customer-unfriendly, and molasses-slow to innovate. In education, more spending has led to flat results. Meanwhile, in the Catholic schools in most inner cities, where the public schools are tragically the worst, a child can get a better education at HALF the cost in the Catholic school system. In New York City, per-child spending is now nearly $40,000—to pay for dismal results. Trump wants a competition model in education (and healthcare) that will revolutionize how we get our healthcare and how we choose our schools.

Trump and the GOP platform has endorsed universal school choice for ALL children regardless of income or ethnicity or race.

8. Promote Free and Fair Trade Deals

Trump believes that the United States is frequently abused when it comes to international trade deals. He has told us first hand that he "uses tariffs as a weapon" to incentivize nations to play fair, but also to promote other American economic and national security objectives. In many case—including arranging deals with China, Japan, Europe and Mexico—that tariff weapon policy has worked. He has transformed the trade relationship with China, with a focus on stopping cheating, stealing, and other misbehavior.

Trump used the threat of tariffs and other penalties against our trading partners to reduce IP theft and force nations like Japan and China to open up their markets. It is a dangerous game, and it is a highly unconventional approach to trade policy, but one that has broad support throughout the country.

Trump has proposed a 10% across the board tariff and a special tariff of up to 60% on imports from China.

9. Downsize Government

Under Joe Biden and his $6 trillion spending spree, government spending has now reached 40% of our GDP. We are moving inexorably toward a socialist country.

Trump tried to enact real spending constraints when he was President. His first two budgets requested a massive downsizing of government with the cancellation of scores of spending programs that are no longer necessary or cost-effective, if they ever were. Trump also endorsed the "Penny Plan"—cut one cent of spending for every dollar an agency receives for each of five years. After a decade, this simple formula would balance the budget.

But Trump didn't have great success in reducing spending. Some of that is because his spending restraint goals were ignored by Congress. And spending also exploded because of the Covid-19 pandemic—a once in a half-century crisis. His average annual deficits were $750 billion—which were way too high, but only half the $1.5 trillion deficits under Biden.

In his second term, Trump and his economic team have identified hundreds of billions of dollars of waste, fraudulent payments (as in the Covid programs), unspent funds that could be returned to the Treasury, and a $350 billion green energy slush fund that should be returned to taxpayers.

10. Create a National Commission on Government Waste

Trump has also suggested a new Grace Commission (modeled after the famous blue-ribbon panel convened by Ronald Reagan in 1981) that would bring together top experts from the private sector in business, management and logistics to find ways to reform our government and reduce costs, waste, redundancy and obsolescence. This could save hundreds of billions without reducing vital services to Americans.

11. Empower the President with Impoundment Authority

Every president from Thomas Jefferson through Richard Nixon used impoundment to stop billions of dollars in unnecessary spending. FDR used the power to switch the U.S. economy over to a wartime economy by slashing through impoundment authority to cancel unneeded spending. Trump wants an impoundment authority or a line item veto to prevent a debt crisis in the years to come.

12. Implement a Pro-America Immigration Policy

Overshadowed by Trump's call for a border wall and some cuts in our family-based immigration system was his call for a "merit-based immigration system." This visa system would select immigrants based on their skills, talents, investment capital, English-language ability, and education level. These characteristics all presage success in America. We used to tell Trump that these immigrants are very desirable because they are the world's "brainiacs."

Given that almost all international migrants want to choose the United States as their destination, this new merit system could create dozens of new Silicon Valley tech centers across the country, giving the United States a giant advantage over China, Germany, Canada, and other nations that want to challenge American economic and industrial superiority. These immigrants are more likely than American-born citizens to create new businesses, new patents, and new American-made consumer products. The United States would still allow immediate family members—spouses and children—to gain visas, but most others would be chosen based on how they will benefit the United States.

13. Revive American's Great Cities Through Enterprise Zones

Our once-great cities in America—from New York to Chicago to Detroit to San Francisco to Seattle—have come to look like war zones. Crime has run rampant. Businesses and people and capital are fleeing and leaving the poorest Americans—mostly minorities stranded with tragically limited opportunities other than working at Walmart or McDonalds for minimum wage. Since 2020 our major cities have lost nearly one million residents. New York City alone lost more than 420,000 residents from 2020 through 2022.[7] And tens of thousands of businesses have been shut down nationwide.

Trump wants to revitalize our cities and abandoned rural areas through deregulation, reduction in tax rates, changes in zoning policies and infrastructure investments to make American cities great again.

14. Eliminate Taxes on Social Security Benefits

Donald Trump has proposed that Social Security benefits should not be taxed. Just as with the Trump idea earlier this summer to

7 https://www.census.gov/library/stories/2023/05/large-cities-no-longer-biggest-population-losers.html

not taxing tips, Democrats are publicly objecting and privately wondering: why didn't we think of this ourselves?

Currently Social Security recipients with incomes below $25,000 individually or $32,000 for couples are exempt entirely from the tax. Those with higher incomes can get taxed on up to 85% of their benefits received. This is a big disincentive to work. It's also unfair to seniors who do continue to work after age 65.

About half of seniors on Social Security pay taxes on their benefits because of other income. That's millions of seniors ensnared in this tax.

As the system currently works, the government takes about 12.6 percent of each worker's paycheck through a payroll tax. Then the government pays a small benefit worth less than half of what workers paid in (plus a fair rate of return) when the worker retires. The average benefit is around $2,000 a month—loosely dependent on how much that person paid in and how much they worked. (By the way: who can live on $2,000 a month?)

A big benefit of the Trump proposal is that it rewards seniors for continuing to work and invest. Right now the tax on working for seniors can be well over 50 percent or more of their paycheck. This is because they pay regular income tax on the earning plus the tax on the benefits.

This policy change is also a matter of fairness. When grandma and grandpa retire, they shouldn't have so much of their earnings taxed away. Nor should they be taxed yet again when the die.

15. End Taxes on Tips

President Trump comes from the hotel business, the building trades, and service industries where the workers get paid with tips. He understands that tips are vital income to car parkers, waiters, waitresses, chefs, bartenders, hotel workers and home repair workers, delivery truck drivers—to name a few. These are service workers who have been harmed by Bidenflation. What better way to reward the best workers, than by making their tips tax-free? This is a better idea than hiring tens of thousands of new IRS agents.

16. Pull the U.S. Out of the Paris Climate Change Treaty and Other Anti-America Treaties

Trump has vowed to end American participation in globalist treaties that hurt America most. This includes the Paris climate accord—a treaty that most other nations have failed to comply with and yet places huge burdens on American companies and workers. Trump also has pledged to end global taxation—such as Janet Yellen's global minimum tax.

17. Drain the Swamp

There is a reason that three of the five wealthiest counties in America are in or around Washington, D.C. Washington is getting rich at the expense of the rest of us. Only 6% of overpaid federal workers (of which there are more than 2 million) are working fulltime in the office. This is despite that Covid ended three years not showing up. Trump has pledged to cut the size of the federal workforce and continue to move federal agencies outside of the Washington swamp—which too often is really a hot tub.

It's a giant rip off of the American taxpayer.

Trump understands that our $7 trillion federal enterprise has become completely alienated from the concerns and needs of the American people. They work for us—but the federal bureaucrats act as if we work for them.

TRUMPONOMICS 2.0 WILL MAKE AMERICA GREAT AGAIN

These ideas have—predictably already generated fierce resistance from the statists.

But it's worth nothing at the outset that Trumponomics encountered ferocious resistance by the left. This is hardly a surprise: the philosophy of Trumponomics assaults the basic framework of command-and-control policies, globalism, the righteousness of the political class, and the victimization thesis of modern-day liberalism. That's why these reforms in the way our arrogant government operates are so urgently needed.

We have agreed with most principles of Trumpism and most of Trump's reforms. We had differences with him in areas such as immigration and trade. And we tried to persuade him to veto spending bills when he was president, which we regarded as obese and economically unwise. He has told us subsequently that he wishes he'd taken our advice on some of those "omnibus" spending bills. We hope he will be more tightfisted the next time around.

On the big-picture priorities—the major reforms that need to be made to our government—it was our belief in 2016, and remains so today, that Trump had the right political and economic take on what ails America and how to fix things. Trumponomics was the right game plan and Trump was the right man to sell it. History is about to repeat itself. When Trump returns to the Oval Office in January of 2025, our bet is that prosperity will make a grand comeback, and America will experience, to borrow a phrase from John F. Kennedy: "a rising tide of prosperity that lifts all boats."

CHAPTER 7

Kamala-tastrophe!

In the few weeks before this book was sent off to printing, Democrats threw Joe Biden off the side of their ship and handed the reins over to Vice President Kamala Harris (a candidate who never received a single primary vote). From a policy point of view, it doesn't matter much which of these two are at the top of the ticket because Biden and Harris are attached at the hip on policy.

Kamala hasn't distanced herself from Bidenomics. She has praised it to the hilt as an enormous success. As mentioned previously, she provided the tie-breaking votes in the Senate for some $3 trillion of spending—for both the "Build Back Better" legislation and the so-called "Inflation Reduction Act." She owns Biden's record whether she likes it or not.

She has promised four more years for more of the same agenda—though possibly a more radical one. Can the U.S. economy withstand this kind of assault?

We've learned over many decades that the American economy is amazingly and even heroically resilient. But there are only so many body-blows it can absorb. That's the painful historical lesson from the Great Depression of the 1930s and the stagflation of the 1970s, when high inflation, high tax rates, the vast expansion of the welfare state, and burgeoning government costs crushed the middle and lower classes.

This chapter tries to answer the question: What if Kamala Harris wins the election?

Will she move to the middle? Will she unify the country? Will she work to erase some of the profound policy errors that we highlighted above?

It's too early to tell, and we profoundly wish we could say the answer to these questions is yes. Will she govern as a JFK/ Bill Clinton pro-business and pro-free market Democrat? Or will she govern from the far left as was the case under Obama and Biden?

Alas, her entire reelection campaign has been a pledge to double down on the failed policies of increased regulation, spending, debt and illegal immigration. Worse, if we look at her actual voting record and the far-out-in-outer-space policy positions, it's hard to be anything but horrified at the prospect of a Harris presidency coming on top of the failures of Bidenomics.

We hear our friends say that we will have Barack Obama's fourth term if Harris wins. That's scary enough, but we think it's more likely we are facing a Bernie Sanders/Elizabeth Warren socialist agenda. It is not a promise to drain the swamp, but to pump trillions more of your and our money into it. She is a San Francisco Democrat through and through. And God forbid that we make America look like the once-great American city of San Francisco—ruined by progressive governance.

Did we mention that while Kamala Harris was in the United States Senate she tallied a MORE liberal voting record than Bernie Sanders and Elizabeth Warren?

WELCOME TO KAMALA-NOMICS

Here's a preview of what Kamala Harris has in store for the country. It isn't a pretty picture and could easily shipwreck the American economy if these policies came to pass. Buckle up you seat belt and we will give you a ride through Kamala-world. Many of these far-left policies are documented on https://www.atr.org/kamalanomics/.

1) Another $2 Trillion Spending Spree

   To their credit, Republicans in Congress were able to stop some of the Biden agenda. There is still roughly $2 trillion of Biden's social welfare and climate change agenda that the Democrats are likely to put at the top of the docket in 2025 if they sweep the White House, Senate and House.

THE LEVER

Most of Biden's Social Agenda Never Materialized

The IRA dropped $1.7 trillion of the funding in the Build Back Better Act

	Build Back Better Act (House-passed version)	Inflation Reduction Act (enacted version)
Climate	$560B	$369B
Child care & universal pre-K	$380B	$0
Paid family/medical leave	$205B	$0
Child tax credit	$190B	$0
Affordable housing	$175B	$0
Medicaid home/community care	$150B	$0
ACA subsidies	$120B	$64B
Immigration reform	$110B	$0
Education/workforce aid	$40B	$0
Medicare hearing coverage	$35B	$0
Other spending	$190B	$4B

DATA: CBO, CRFB, U.S. SENATE, JOINT COMMITTEE ON TAXATION
ANALYSIS: STEPHEN SEMLER (@STEPHENSEMLER) FOR THE LEVER (@LEVERNEWS). DESIGN: LINDSAY BALLANT/THE LEVER

https://www.levernews.com/bidenomics-isnt-working-for-working-people/

2) The Harris Tax Hike Assault

Harris has called for a radical redistribution of income through massive tax hikes on American companies, investors, and employers. The tax rates she has proposed would be higher than in Russian and China. No country in world history has ever gotten rich by raising tax rates, but many have sunk their economies by doing that.

As we've mentioned in previous chapters, Harris and the congressional Democrats have made it clear they want to repeal the entire Trump tax cut. They also support some of the largest tax increases in American history on investment and business creation.

Here is a short list of the Biden plan as outlined in his own documents:

Kamala has signed off on all of these measures as Vice President for Biden. Like Biden, Kamala has put forward no other idea on how to balance the budget other than to raise taxes. The plan, if adopted, would be the largest increase in taxes and tax rates, in history. The plan would:

- Raise the corporate tax rate to 28%, higher than Communist China and Russia.
- Impose a global corporate minimum tax of 21%.
- Deny corporations a tax deduction when they pay over $1 million to any employee.
- Quadruple the stock buyback tax (we told you it wouldn't stay at 1%), which will undermine returns for all investors.

- Impose a new 25% tax on unrealized capital gains on "billionaires," defined as anyone with wealth of $100 million, which is less than a billion.

These tax hikes would pay for a massive expansion of welfare spending in the tax code with advanceable "child credit" monthly checks for non-taxpayers, increases in the earned income credit, and a permanent extension of supersized Obamacare subsidies.

The full plan is here:

https://www.whitehouse.gov/briefing-room/statements-releases/2024/03/07/fact-sheet-president-biden-is-fighting-to-reduce-the-deficit-cut-taxes-for-working-families-and-invest-in-america-by-making-big-corporations-and-the-wealthy-pay-their-fair-share/

The irony of course is that the high taxes on the rich will crush economic growth but are likely to reduce their tax share, just as the Trump tax cuts increased it.

3) A "Net Zero" Energy Policy Eliminating Production of America's Abundant Fossil Fuels

    America and the rest of the world still generate roughly 80% of our energy from old-fashioned oil, gas, coal and diesel. There is no mythical "green energy" transition, as the chart below shows:

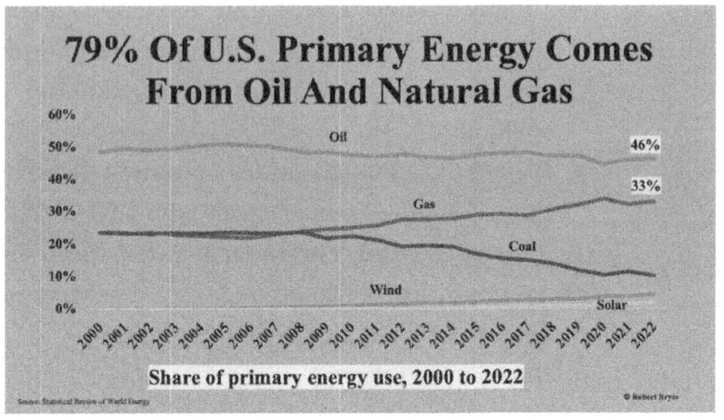

Yet Kamala has said: "There is no question that I am in favor of banning fracking." She has also supported a carbon tax—which would be equivalent to an extra sales tax on most goods and services that we buy—even if you make less than $400,000.

She's also fully committed to net zero fossil Fuels and getting nearly all of our energy from the electric grid system via windmills, switch grass, and solar panel—all 19th century forms of energy. That a technological pipedream, requiring a doubling of the electric grid system that is already experiencing brown outs in States like California. It would also make our entire $24 trillion economy dependent on one source. The cost of heating your home would likely double or triple.

Worst of all, the net zero agenda means that nearly all American energy production would come to a screeching halt and we would become almost entirely dependent on other nations for our energy generation.

4) An End to State Right to Work Laws in 26 States

Kamala is a strong and vocal supporters of a bill called the pro-union "PRO Act," which would overturn more than half-a century of labor law.

The union bosses tried mightily to push this law over the goal line in 2021—but thankfully they fell a few votes short. The Pro Act would repeal right to work laws in the 26 mostly red states. Right to work would be replaced with a universal "closed shop" forced union policy. This would mean that businesses, shops, and factories that have fled to red states like Florida and Texas would move operations overseas. Millions of American workers would be required to join a union and pay union dues in order to keep their jobs. They would have to see their union dues paid for political campaigns against their will and even when they don't support the candidates the union bosses have selected.

This is a blatant violation of First Aamendment rights of freedom of association. Americans should never have to forfeit their fundamental rights as citizens to get and hold up to their job. Right-to-work states create jobs at twice the rate of forced-union states.

5) Antitrust Regulations Would Jeopardize America's High Tech Global Domination

We've seen the craziness of FTC chair Lina Kahn, who wants to effectively eliminate all mergers and acquisitions in industries ranging from social media, search engines, software, video streaming, cell phones, artificial intelligence, and online retail transactions. In each of these industries, prices are not rising. They are rapidly falling. This regulation assault will raise prices for consumers, dramatically slow innovation, and cripple the ability of start-up businesses to raise capital, thus putting America's multi-trillions of dollars of global tech dominance in grave danger. This couldn't be coming at a worse time now that we are in a battle to win the race for the next generation of artificial intelligence technologies, robotics, and human-genome related cures for diseases.

6) A Government Takeover of the Health Care System

Many readers will remember when Barack Obama famously declared: "Under my plan, if you like your health plan you can keep it." He wasn't being honest since millions of Americans have been pushed into government plans. But Kamala doesn't want you to have choices.

Health care policy expert Avik Roy has tracked down Kamala's declarations on health care over the years and they are unambiguous. She supports Medicare for All, which would abolish employer plans for tens of millions of Americans.

If you don't believe us, here is a good summary of her declarations on health care as well summarized in Forbes.com:

Kamala Harris was the first senator to co-sponsor Bernie Sanders' bill, the Medicare for All Act of 2017. "Here, I'll break some news," she said that year at a town hall in Oakland, California. "I intend to co-sponsor the Medicare-for-all bill, because it's just the right thing to do." 15 other Democrats eventually joined her.

That bill, if enacted, would have abolished private health insurance for all age groups (including Medicare beneficiaries) and replaced it with a government-run single-payer system to benefit "every individual who is a resident of the United States," including undocumented immigrants. (Bernie Sanders has popularized the term "Medicare for all" for a U.S. version of single-payer, government-run health insurance.)

On January 21, 2019, Harris announced that she was seeking the 2020 Democratic nomination for President. A few days later, at a CNN town hall in Iowa, she elaborated on why she sought to eliminate private insurance. In response to a questioner who asked her if her health care solution "involved cutting insurance companies as we know them out of the equation," Harris agreed, saying, "I believe the solution—and I actually feel very strongly about this—is that we need to have Medicare for all. That's just the bottom line...it is inhumane to make people go through a system where they cannot literally receive the benefit of what medical science can offer because some insurance company has decided it doesn't meet their bottom line."

CNN host Jake Tapper followed up, asking, "You're also a co-sponsor onto [the Medicare for all bill]. I believe it will totally eliminate private insurance. So for people out there who like their insurance, they don't get to keep it?" Harris responded:

> Well, listen, the idea is that everyone gets access to medical care, and you don't have to go through the process of going through an insurance company, having them give you approval, going through the paperwork, all of the delay that may require. Who of us has not had that situation, where you've got to wait for approval, and the doctor says, well, I don't know if your insurance company is going to cover this? *Let's eliminate all of that. Let's move on.* [Emphasis added.]

Amazingly, even her Democratic challengers trashed the idea as crazy. Michael Bloomberg charged: "To replace the entire private system where companies provide health care for their employees would bankrupt us for a very long time." Truer words were never spoken.

Kamala has now backtracked from her absurd Medicare for All position, but will she change her mind on January 21, 2025 if she wins the election?

7) Make Washington, D.C. and Puerto Rico states in order to gain four more seats in the Senate.

   Kamala supports statehood and we know why. The Democrats want to forever retain control of the Senate so there is no way that Republicans can block their agenda.

8) Repeal the filibuster in the Senate. The filibuster requires 60 votes to pass major legislation, which is a

safeguard against racing to pass unwise legislation without proper analysis and consensus. The Senate is supposed to be the world's most deliberative body. It protects against mob rule. Democrats want to trample the rights of the minority by allowing all major legislation to pass the Senate with a simple 51 seat majority. This would trample the rights of the minority party.

9) Pack the Supreme Court with 3 to 5 additional justices to swing the majority in their direction.
10) End the Electoral College and institute a national popular vote. This would take power away from the states—especially the smaller states—and encourage massive voter fraud in all the major cities.
11) Allow illegal immigrants to vote and allow all noncitizens voting rights. We know this is part of the plan because nearly all Senate and House Republicans voted against proof of citizenship to vote. Kamala and the Democrats also support "automatic voter registration" so that illegal immigrants and other noncitizens can vote without showing proof of citizenship. We view this as a PARAMOUNT assault on Democracy.
12) Ban or regulate gas cars, air conditioners, gas heat, SUVs, and scores of other home appliances and travel conveniences, while regulating the thermostat in people's homes. This may seem Orwellian, but all these ideas are on the table and under discussion among Democrat big thinkers. Biden and Kamala have approved regulations that would ban the production of gas cars within 10 to 15 years. Remember: Kamala was the author of a California policy to ban plastic

straws. That mentality has given birth to the era of paper straws that don't work.

13) Implement racial preferences in hiring and application for colleges and schools. Democrats have abandoned the notion of a colorblind society. In fact, they think "colorblind" is a racist term. The new movement in the progressive movement/Democratic party is DEI: Diversity, Equity and Inclusion—code word for quotas.
14) Confiscate the wealth of higher income families by taxing unrealized capital gains and instituting new wealth taxes. All of this will be justified in the name of "fairness" and "equality."

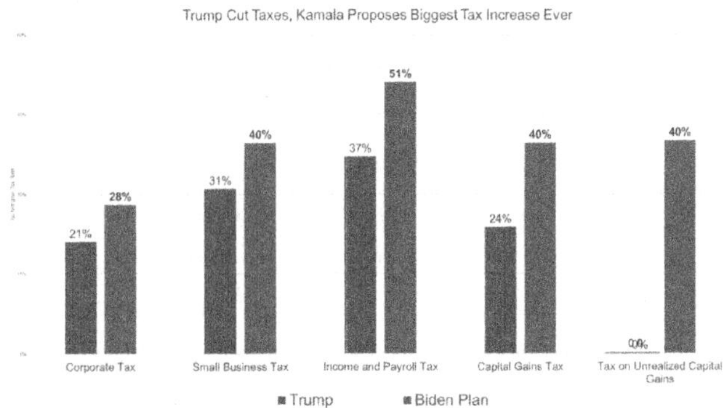

15) Implement failed government price controls on everything from rents, to drugs, to housing, to internet services. Kamala and Biden support bringing back discredited and unworkable price controls to try to lower the prices of the goods and services that their own spending and debt bombs caused in the first place. But almost all economists agree that the only

effect of price controls is to make consumers worse off by inciting shortages. Jason Furman, the chair of the Council of Economic Advisers under President Obama, recently said that "rent control has been about as disgraced as any economic policy in the tool kit. The idea we'd be reviving and expanding it will ultimately make our housing supply problems worse, not better." So naturally, that's what Kamala wants to do.

OUR FREE ENTERPRISE SYSTEM IS IN GRAVE DANGER

We wish we could say that we are exaggerating the threats that Kamala Harris poses to our economic progress and our basic liberties.

Sorry. No. These threats are very real and reflect the far-left takeover of the Democratic party. Kamala Harris doesn't strike us as one who thought very deeply about any of these issues or the ramifications of her proposals. She's transactional in her politics and her policies and tends to default to the doctrinaire and most radical positions of the party to make sure no one can get to the left of her. The American vision of our nation as a land of equal opportunity for all, will be slowly shifted to a nation of equal outcomes. And history proves that the end result of absolute equality by taxing the rich and giving to the poor and giving power to government to achieve these ends, always and invariably leads to everyone being poorer. It is the surest path to tyranny.

Beware.

TRUMP'S ROAD BACK TO THE WHITE HOUSE

As we write this, three months before election day, Donald Trump is leading or tied in most national polls. But that isn't the reason we expect Donald Trump to be elected President this November. After all, Trump was LOSING in nearly every poll in 2016 until he won the poll that matters on election day. The primary reason Trump will win—other than that the economy performed so much better during the Trump presidency than the Biden presidency—is that Trump is a winner. He almost always wins.

THE LOOK OF A WINNER

We've often said that there have been five politicians in our lifetimes that have won over the hearts and minds of the American people in a compelling way. They spoke to Americans' aspirations and had a charisma, charm, and connection with the American people that was impressive to behold.

Those five:

John F. Kennedy
Ronald Reagan

Bill Clinton
Barack Obama
Donald J. Trump

Whether you agreed or disagreed with their policies—they were great "politicians" and "leaders" in many ways. We weren't fans of Barack Obama's policies but the fact that he was the country's first black president and gave hope to so many millions of minority families was a wonderful thing for our country.

Kennedy and Reagan were optimistic and wholesome and patriotic unifiers of the country. They both played pivotal roles in winning the Cold War and reinstating Americans' faith in our nation. Clinton was a young charmer who spoke to a new generation of voters and successfully moved the Democratic party to the middle and accomplished some great things: a balanced budget, a booming stock market, welfare reform, and an era of peace and prosperity.

Trump has that X factor of connecting with the American middle class and relating to their fears, their aspirations and their love of country. This is why "Make America Great Again" remains such a powerful and popular theme for our country. Biden dourly speaks of all the things that are wrong with America and Americans; Trump trumpets what is right.

We would highlight two similarities of these five successful Presidents. First, they loved people. They loved the voters. And second, they were ALWAYS underestimated. JFK was a young kid running for president against a seasoned veteran in Richard Nixon. He couldn't win. Reagan was continually written off as "too old," too conservative, and too dangerous in his views on the world. Clinton was a guy with a nice smile from Hope, Arkansas, but far too unseasoned and raw to be president of the United States. Barack Obama could never win because the country wasn't ready to elect a black president with a funny name. And Donald Trump was a bombastic TV personality who sometimes said crazy things that would never go over with the American electorate. He was given a one in one hundred chance of being elected President when he first came down the escalator in Trump Tower.

Here's why we like his chances this time.

THE CHOICE BEFORE US

In some ways the election will be a middle-class voter/jury verdict on Biden and Kamala's handling of the economy. But not just that. Voters are frustrated and angry not just because Biden/Harris have weakened the economy. They've divided the country. It's hard to believe that Biden and Harris ran for the White House as unifiers. We are hard-pressed to think of a single issue that Biden has pursued to unite the country. Instead, he has embraced a far-left agenda on the economy and cultural issue like immigration and race, and that agenda has widened the chasm between left and right.

Kamala chose Tim Walz as his running mate. So now we have at the top of the ticket the most liberal Senator and her VP choice one of the three or four most liberal governors in Minnesota Governor Tim Walz. We all this the left and leftist ticket and the most anti-business ticket of a major party in our lifetimes. Walz is the governor who not only locked down his businesses, schools, and churches for more than six months during Covid, but instituted a government phone hotline encouraging Minnesotans to rat on their neighbors if they violated social distancing rules.

Admittedly, Trump sometimes fails to unite the country and sometimes he uses rhetoric that needlessly offends people. We wish he wouldn't.

But one key difference between these two candidates is that Trump celebrates America's greatness and Biden highlights—often in unpatriotic ways—America's flaws. Biden has even on many occasions referred to the United States as being infected with "systemic racism,"[8] which is what our adversaries say about America. Who would ever think this outrageous and untruthful slur would be repeated by our president. "Blame America First" is hardly a winning message for an electorate that loves our country despite our national failings. Harris is even more pronounced in playing the race card in a divisive "us versus them" way.

As we noted in our previous book, *Trumponomics*, Trump's strategy in 2016 was to energize and grow his base of conservative and independent populist voters by emphasizing economic growth, tax cuts, illegal immigration controls, building out our infrastructure, lowering debt spending, drilling for American energy, saving the coal industry, and repealing unpopular trade laws. He's running on a similar agenda in 2024, with two added benefits this time around: First, he has a proven track record that the policies worked. And second, he is competing against Kamala Harris and the modern "progressive Democratic party," which has started to implement these policy prescriptions. They've almost all failed to deliver as promised. We think voters are likely to respond to this litany of misfired policies with a clear message: "return to sender."

---

8 https://www.whitehouse.gov/briefing-room/speeches-remarks/2021/01/26/remarks-by-president-biden-at-signing-of-an-executive-order-on-racial-equity/

Trump breezed through the Republican primaries. He won every one of them where he was on the ballot, by a wide margin, despite not participating in any of the Republican debates. Some of the candidates embraced him, some rejected him, and some tried to split the difference. But none of it mattered—Trump defeated them all. He has unified the party in an impressive way and has rallied the support of his two chief rivals in the primaries: Florida governor Ron DeSantis and former South Carolina governor Nikki Haley.

Democrats have begun to wage a nasty fight against him and have run mudslinging multi-million-dollar campaign ads accusing him of being a racist and other vulgar characterizations. They've dug up things that Trump said 10, 15, or 20 years ago and twisted them out of context. They say he supported white nationalism when he was president.

Here's the problem. Trump already has a record on race. It is one of the best EVER of any president—as we showed earlier in this book. Under Trump, black incomes rose in real terms more than any other president in modern times—while blacks LOST ground under Biden. Under Trump, the black poverty rate fell to its lowest level EVER. Under Trump, the black unemployment rate fell to its lowest level EVER under Trump. All of these achievements were also true during Trump's first term when applied to Hispanics.

How can a president who did more for black economic and financial advancement than any president in our lifetimes be a racist? This absurd claim reveals how desperate the Democrats and Biden have become—like an angry trapped rattle snake in the corner ready to snap at anyone who comes close.

When it comes to the Electoral College, Harris has big states like California and New York in the bag (though New York could be surprisingly close). These two states are very likely to deliver Biden 82 of the needed 270 Electoral College votes. Trump has two big red states firmly supporting him, Florida and Texas, and they account for 70 electoral votes.

Most other states are not going to be highly contested, which means the election is likely to be decided by the following six states: Arizona, Georgia, Michigan, Nevada, Pennsylvania, and Wisconsin. A handful of other states are also in play. Trump could win Minnesota, Nevada, and New Hampshire—all of which are close. If it is a wave election, Trump could also bag Maine, New Jersey, New Mexico. Trump has a strong populist foot hold in each of these traditionally blue states.

While each of those states are very different, they are all made up of a solid working class (most of whom do not have a college degree) and are often times marginal voters. Trump drives millions of these marginal voters—the forgotten Americans—in ways that few politicians have done in recent decades. These working-class voters are drawn to his Make America Great Again message, as well as focus on expanding the economy for everyone, not a privileged few. They also have almost no interest in the left's three primary issues: LGBTQ+, climate change, and race.

Trump's a larger-than-life personality, of course, and his baggage—such as the January 6, 2021, Capitol riot and the lawsuit involving Stormy Daniels—will be invoked constantly by the left.

But here are a few of the issues that we believe tip the race in Trump's favor.

Immigration

We believe as economists that LEGAL immigration is beneficial to America. But illegal immigration is out of control and the border is so full of holes it could be a slice of swiss cheese.

Trump made a crackdown on illegal immigration a centerpiece of his 2016 campaign. And he's never been shy about sharing his thoughts about illegal immigrants and the harm they're doing to the United States. While we've traditionally been supporters of increased *legal* immigration, and haven't been as focused on the illegal side, we understand why illegal immigration and border security resonates with voters.

A national *Wall Street Journal* poll conducted in late February of 2024 found that 20 percent of voters identified immigration as their top issue. That was more than any other issue in the poll. Strikingly, 65 percent of those polled said they didn't approve of the way in which Biden was dealing with border security. An ABC News poll showed that his approval rating on immigration was just 18 percent—the lowest the poll had recorded in 20 years of asking the question.[9]

In the six swing states listed above, plus North Carolina, another *Wall Street Journal* poll revealed widespread dissatisfaction with the country's immigration and policy and border security. The *lowest* share of voters dissatisfied in those was 72 percent. In all seven of those states, immigration was either the most important, or second most important, issue for voters. And Trump's approach was favored over Biden's by 14 percentage points.[10] That's going to make it very difficult for Harris to pre-

---

9 https://www.langerresearch.com/wp-content/uploads/1231a2IntotheElection-.pdf

10 https://www.wsj.com/politics/elections/election-2024-immigration-issue-voters-84916a17

vail, given her role as the "border czar" under President Biden and given that Trump's approach will be a stimulus for people who agree with his position to vote.

"Every town is now a border town because Joe Biden/Kamala Harris have brought the carnage and chaos and killing from all over the world and dumped it straight into our backyards," says Trump. Americans are feeling the pain.

Kamala hasn't even attempted to control the border. In just one month—February 2024—there were more than 140,000 arrests at the southern border, according to the federal government's own figures.[11] But we also know that hundreds of thousands of undocumented immigrants have found a way into the United States. That has even led the mayors of some so-called "sanctuary" cities to plead with the federal government for relief. Eric Adams, the mayor of New York, said in September 2023 that the surge of immigrants "will destroy New York City."[12] All of this plays into Trump's hands, since he's spent years calling for a border wall to be built and for tighter enforcement of immigration laws.

The support for a crackdown on illegal immigration spans both parties. An Axios poll published in April 2024 showed that while 68 percent of Republicans favored mass deportations of illegal immigrants, so did 42 percent of Democrats.[13] That's not the story you'll hear in the media, but it is another reason why Trump is favored to win in November.

---

11 https://www.cbp.gov/newsroom/national-media-release/cbp-releases-february-2024-monthly-update

12 https://www.nytimes.com/2023/09/07/nyregion/adams-migrants-destroy-nyc.html

13 https://www.axios.com/2024/04/25/trump-biden-americans-illegal-immigration-poll

Biden and Harris have taken a soft line on illegal immigration in no small part because they see immigrants as a potential voting bloc that can deliver them to victory. The authors of a 2013 report from the Center for American Progress, a liberal think tank, wrote: "Supporting real immigration reform that contains a pathway to citizenship for our nation's 11 million undocumented immigrants is the only way to maintain electoral strength in the future."[14] That's a deeply cynical—and reckless—approach to immigration, and it's infected the Biden administration's policies.

This is the cynical and illegal plot we call "Let 'Em In and Let 'Em Vote" strategy by the Democrats as they search for the votes they need to win in November. With six to eight million added illegal immigrants in the country under Biden, there are a lot of potential illegal votes to be had.

If this seems overly conspiratorial, consider that cities such as San Francisco and New York have recently sought to allow non-citizens the right to vote, claiming they deserve to participate in decision-making. Starting this year, Washington, D.C. will allow ANY adult who has been a resident for 30 days and claims they don't vote anywhere else, to vote in local elections. That includes illegal immigrants. A federal court voted to allow this!

Then in a vote in the U.S. House of Representatives, 143 House Democrat Reps voted NOT TO OVERTURN the DC law.

Illegal immigrant voting is a clear and present danger. The website Just Facts concluded this year that:

- non-citizens have ample openings to illegally vote.
- roughly 10% to 27% of them are registered to vote.

---

14 https://www.americanprogress.org/article/immigration-is-changing-the-political-landscape-in-key-states/

- about 5% to 13% of them vote in presidential elections.[15]

While it is illegal for all non-citizens to vote in federal elections, enforcement is variable at best. If only 10% of the illegal immigrants in swing states are voting, this could decide the election.

When the House and Senate voted on a bill called the SAFE ACT to require voters to show proof of citizenship before casting their vote, Democrats almost all voted no. They say it was too much of a burden placed on the voter. So you can vote without an ID, but you can't board a plane or cash a check without one.

Can you think of a greater "danger to our democracy?"

Hispanics

The standard liberal retort to Trump's tough love approach to illegal immigration is that it's going to depress his popularity among immigrants—particularly Hispanics—who now account for about 15 percent of the U.S. population.

But once again, the left and its allies in the punditocracy are all wrong. The reality is that many immigrants who waited in line, and came to the United States legally, support cracking down on those who came illegally. As Monica De La Cruz, a Republican congresswoman, points out, "We witness 10 million people breaking our immigration laws and cutting ahead of our relatives and friends who have waited years to come here legally."[16]

The numbers jump around, but a *New York Times* poll released in March 2024 found that Trump had become more pop-

---

15 https://www.justfacts.com/news_non-citizen_voter_registration

16 https://www.newsweek.com/trump-gaining-latinos-because-he-delivered-america-dream-opinion-1874940

ular than Biden among Hispanics, by a 46-40 margin.[17] This has confounded Democrats, who want to portray Hispanics (and all other ethnic and racial groups) as victims of white oppression.

Hispanics see America as a land of opportunity, which is why they wanted to come to this country. And they've already been gravitating to Trump. He received a higher share of the Hispanic vote in Florida, Texas, and California in the 2020 election than he did four years earlier—and his overall share rose from 28 percent to 36 percent. Perhaps most revealing, he won a majority of the votes in Texas's heavily-Hispanic Zapata County, which had not voted Republican in a presidential election in 100 years.

The reality is that Hispanics are no different from other Americans in that they're concerned about the kitchen table issues that affect us all. UnidosUS, a Hispanic-focused advocacy group, found that 64 percent of Hispanics surveyed identified an economic issue as their top concern, with inflation and the rising cost of living coming out on top, followed by jobs and the economy.[18]

Economic concerns particularly acute among working-class Hispanics, who account for 78 percent of the Hispanic population. Two-thirds of them, according to a 2024 poll, feel that "inflation is still a very serious problem that is not improving." That's also how 49 percent of college-educated Hispanics

---

17 https://www.nytimes.com/2024/03/02/us/politics/trumps-support-among-latinos-grows-new-poll-shows.html

18 https://unidosus.org/press-releases/unidosus-launches-latino-vote-briefing-series-with-a-deep-dive-on-latino-voters-economic-concerns/

think. And 70 percent of working-class Hispanics identify as moderate-to-conservative.[19]

All of this spells trouble for Kamala in November. As the *New York Times* has pointed out, Trump doesn't even need a majority of Hispanics to support him in order to win the presidential election: "Merely peeling off a few percentage points among the group could prove decisive."[20]

Blacks

There's been a similar shift to Trump among black voters. Polling in April 2024 showed Trump with 18 percent support among blacks, twice the level from the same period in 2016. And polls by ABC, NBC, and CNN showed that among black voters 44 and younger, support ranged from 20 percent to 32 percent. Democrats hope that having Kamala now at the ticket will help drive out black turnout. And they may be right.

But a fundamental issue for blacks has been the weakness of the U.S. economy under Biden/Harris—and the impact of inflation, which hit blacks (and Hispanics) harder than other groups, according to a study the New York Federal Reserve.[21] The *New York Times* poll found 41 percent of blacks rating the economy as "poor" and another 40 percent said "only fair." A *Washington Post* poll released in April 2024 found 49 percent of blacks surveyed saying that Biden's policies had made "no difference" to them. That's one reason why 33 percent of those in the poll said

19 https://d3nkl3psvxxpe9.cloudfront.net/documents/TLP_Wave3_crosstabs.pdf

20 https://www.nytimes.com/2024/03/02/us/politics/trumps-support-among-latinos-grows-new-poll-shows.html

21 https://libertystreeteconomics.newyorkfed.org/2023/01/inflation-disparities-by-race-and-income-narrow/

they were unlikely to vote for Biden, or definitely would not vote for him.[22]

Back to the Economy

We have covered at length "Bidenomics" and the damage the Biden/Harris team has done to the U.S. economy. But it's worth mentioning the political impact of this, since it's going to work in Trump's favor this November.

In a July 2024 Fox News poll in which voters were asked who they preferred to deal with the economy, Trump came out at 52% and Harris at 40%. No poll has shown Kamala even close to Trump on handing the economy.

Polls have now consistently shown that voters trust Trump over Kamala on the economy by 10 to 30 percentage points depending on the pollster. No polls show Kamala better on the economy.

Common Sense Reforms to Make America Great

The far left progressive hijacking of the Democratic party—with the agenda being set by members of the radical "Squad" (including AOC, who opposes business investment even in her own district), the Bernie Sanders socialists, and the radical green climate change agenda—that wants to take away gas cars, gas stoves, and air conditioners—has put Kamala in an embrace of a catalog of policies that are outside the American mainstream.

Liberals still hate law enforcement and want to coddle criminals. Trump stands firmly with the police against the rising tide of lawlessness that has made portions of big cities like Chicago

22 https://www.washingtonpost.com/documents/9d3439ff-4f74-4c0d-b701-7027481140fe.pdf?itid=lk_inline_manual_2

and San Francisco practically unlivable. This is why law enforcement officials are solidly behind Trump.

Kamala is captive to the climate doomsday caucus of the Democratic Party and has pushed a range of policies that have eroded America's competitiveness and undermined the U.S. economy. Trump will reverse these policies—promising to "unleash the production of domestic energy resources, reduce the soaring price of gasoline, diesel and natural gas, promote energy security for our friends around the world, eliminate the socialist Green New Deal and ensure the United States is never again at the mercy of a foreign supplier of energy."[23] That can't happen soon enough.

Trump is against the destructive drug culture, and the loss of any semblance of border control has caused a fentanyl crisis never seen before in our country. Drug deaths have hit an all-time high under Biden/Harris and is causing harm and heartbreak in towns across the country.

Harris has embraced (and Trump opposes) the DEI—diversity, equity, and inclusion—racket that has infected our workplaces, our universities, and even our hospitals. DEI is merely a front for an agenda to impose racial, ethnic and gender identity quotas in the workplace, in board rooms, and in schools and university admissions. Trump favors a color-blind society where individuals are judged by their talents, hard work and achievements, while Biden favors judging Americans by the color of their skin or their gender/sexual orientation.

More generally, Trump doesn't buy into the liberal piety that most of America is motivated by racism and that the only way for racial and ethnic minorities to get ahead is through government-mandated preferences. Similarly, he resists the rising tide

23 https://www.donaldjtrump.com/issues

of transgenderism that school officials support—if not encourage—and that has created confusion among children about the difference between boys and girls.

VOTERS AND THE TRUMP PHENOMENON

We've traveled with Trump across the country during this campaign and it is clear that something big is bubbling up in America. Some 75,000 people showed up in New Jersey, a blue state, to hear Trump's message. He speaks with conviction and says what he means. He was the blue-collar president and is now the blue-collar candidate.

This obvious and genuine affection for Trump by many millions of working-class voters vexes and infuriates the left. After his speech in the Bronx in May—traditional Democratic territory—the excitement and affection that this rainbow coalition of attendees of all ethnicities and young and old was the kind of aroused and spontaneous enthusiasm one sees at a rock concert featuring Bruce Springsteen or Elton John—or even America's sweetheart, Taylor Swift.

Liberal commentators on MSNBC and CNN and reporters from the *New York Times* were truly mystified and appalled. Don't these voters know—they fumed—that Trump is spreading prejudice and divide and hatred.

This response only reinforces our conviction that after all these years, the left still doesn't get Trump or Trumpism. The very political class and the election prognosticators who are supposed to have their finger on the pulse of American voters are estranged from the very electorate that they profess to have under their microscope. We think a major reason why is that Washington, Silicon Valley, Wall Street and the Ivy League faculty lounges live in a bubble of detachment from real America.

These are people who aren't bothered by inflation, gas prices, crime, drug overdoses, boys playing in their daughter's basketball games, campus riots, falling incomes, record credit card debt, unaffordable housing, and a national credit card that now has 12 zeroes.

In 2016, Trump pulled off the most improbable upset in American political history. This year we expect Trump to win by a much wider margin because Americans love peace and prosperity...and America First.

AFTERWORD

The world has changed a lot since we started writing this book in March 2024.

At that time, it seemed that we were destined to see a presidential rematch between Trump and Biden.

We always had our doubts, however. We thought there was a better than 50-50 chance that Democrats would dump Biden—and the only question then would be who would carry the mantle. We always thought that Biden would be thrown off the Democrat express for two reasons: one, his declining mental faculties; and two, his record has been so abysmal it was almost inconceivable that voters would choose four more years.

It turns out that Democrats solved one problem by ousting Biden, but only created another problem by inserting Vice President Kamala Harris. All of our Democrat friends and sources admit that she is a deeply flawed candidate (despite the gushy honeymoon she received from the media in the first weeks when she officially became the nominee), given her staunch statist positions and her failure to achieve the two most important jobs she has been assigned in her political career. As Attorney General in California, she failed to reduce crime—it exploded on her watch. And as Vice President she was assigned the task of

"Border Czar" by President Biden. A fiasco of monumental proportions followed.

Oops. Now voters will decide whether she should be the nation's chief executive and commander in chief.

The other game-changing event for us and the country was the assassination attempt against Donald Trump. For us, this brought on a frightening sense of *déjà vu*.

The two of us remember exactly where we were in March 1981 when we heard the harrowing news that President Ronald Reagan was shot at the entrance of a Hilton Hotel in Washington, D.C. Our hearts sank and we were terrified that a bullet could take away an American president at the start of his administration, when the nation so desperately needed him to fix our country, our economy, our security, our national sense of confidence as "the world's beacon of freedom"—as Reagan himself put it.

No one knew whether Reagan would survive until many hours later. We didn't know how close to death he had come. We only heard his memorable comments before he went into life-threatening surgery: "I just hope you doctors are Republicans."

It could not be his time to be taken away. He had to unleash a global economic expansion. He had to win the Cold War. That was his destiny.

Forty-three later, and a few days before the 2024 Republican convention, where Trump would be nominated for the third time to be the Republican candidate for president, an assassin took aim at him.

The bullet clipped his ear, and we felt the same sense of panic for our friend and for our nation. It is not his time. The nation needs another warrior for free enterprise, prosperity, and American values.

In both cases, the bullet came within an inch of killing the president. Divine intervention? You decide.

A few days after the assassination attempt on Trump, we released a video that you can access at UnleashProsperityNow.com [I don't see the video on the site] The video depicts an iconic scene in the Terminator movie where Arnold Schwarzenegger survives every attempt to kill him. Instead of Arnold walking out of the exploding tunnel, it is Donald Trump. The takeaway line: Donald Trump Is Indestructible.

Whether you love Trump or hate him, we can all agree that he has survived every attempt to destroy him politically. No one in American history has been so shabbily treated or abused by the arrogant media. Think about it:

When he came down the escalator at Trump Tower in late 2015 and announced his presidency, the political experts burst out laughing and said that he was a one-in-a-hundred chance to win.

When he won the presidency in his race against Hillary Clinton the Democrats spent two years on a Russia collusion story that has been discredited.

When his popularity climbed in the wake of his successful policies, the Democrats retaliated by trying to impeach him three times.

When he lost the presidency in 2020, the media experts joyously wrote his political obituary. They said this was finally the end of the road for Donald Trump. He would never win another Republican nomination.

When he decided to run again the Democrats threatened to put him in jail for more than 300 years with sham prosecutions.

When he was on trial in New York, he faced a corrupt judge, a corrupt jury, and a corrupt key witness who testified against him, which led to a highly questionable conviction—almost certain to be overturned.

They keep figuratively firing and firing at him and missing.

Then the man even dodged a real bullet.

The odds are seemingly always stacked up against Trump and yet he soldiers on. He gains strength from his attackers.

In the weeks before this book went to print, the media has been reporting that Wall Street and academic economists and even Nobel prize winners believe a Democrat would be better for the economy than Trump. This entire book has documented how preposterous that claim is given the record of these past two presidents. Trump's critics also are warning that he will cause high inflation, interest rates will skyrocket, the global monetary system will blow up, and American democracy will be destroyed. The New Republic even depicted Trump as Adolph Hitler. Those suffering from Trump Derangement Syndrome can't help themselves.

Many of these predictions of doom may sound familiar because this is exactly what Trump's critics said when he was running for president in 2016 and after he won.

To end this book with a little light-hearted humor, we collected the hysterical predictions that were made in that year.

1) "Donald Trump's first gift to the world will be another financial crisis." Headline in the *Independent*, a London-based newspaper. From the article: "He gives every impression that he will soon be hustling America—and possibly the entire world—in the direction of another catastrophic financial crisis."

2) "I have no stocks. I advise people not to invest in the stock market, not now. Way too dangerous." Filmmaker Michael Moore, August 2017.
3) "It really does now look like President Donald J. Trump, and markets are plunging. When might we expect them to recover? We are very probably looking at a global recession, with no end in sight." Paul Krugman of *The New York Times*, the day after the election.
4) "If Trump wins we should expect a big markdown in expected future earnings for a wide range of stocks—and a likely crash in the broader market." Eric Zitzewitz, former economist with the International Monetary Fund, November 2016.
5) "Under Trump, I would expect a protracted recession to begin within 18 months. The damage would be felt far beyond the United States." Larry Summers, Secretary of the Treasury for Bill Clinton and chief economist for Barack Obama, June 2016.
6) "If the unlikely event happens and Trump wins you will see a market crash of historic proportions, I think.... The markets are terrified of him." Steve Rattner, MSNBC economic guru, October 2016.
7) "Wall Street is set up for a major crash if Donald Trump shocks the world on Election Day and wins the White House. New research suggests that financial markets strongly prefer a Hillary Clinton presidency and could react with panicked selling should Trump deliver a shocking upset on Nov. 8." Ben White, Politico, October 2016.

And finally, and most unambiguously:

8) "A President Trump Could Destroy the World Economy" Headline of a *Washington Post* editorial, October 2016.

Instead, we had prosperity, higher incomes, and a booming stock market.

As Ronald Reagan might have put it: Well, there they go again.

ABOUT THE AUTHORS

Arthur B. Laffer is the legendary founder of supply-side economics and economic advisor to President Ronald Reagan and Prime Minister Margaret Thatcher. He was awarded the Presidential Medal of Freedom by President Donald Trump in 2019.

Stephen Moore is a Senior Economist at FreedomWorks. Previously, Moore served as an economic advisor to President Donald Trump and as a member of the *Wall Street Journal*'s editorial board.

Made in United States
North Haven, CT
28 September 2024

58044739R00114